CIMA Managerial Studies

Be Prepared

CIMA Managerial Studies

Be Prepared

Mike Rogers

ELSEVIER

AMSTERDAM • BOSTON • HEIDELBERG • LONDON
NEW YORK • OXFORD • PARIS • SAN DIEGO
SAN FRANCISCO • SINGAPORE • SYDNEY • TOKYO

CIMA Publishing is an imprint of Elsevier

CIMA
PUBLISHING

CIMA Publishing
An imprint of Elsevier
Linacre House, Jordan Hill, Oxford OX2 8DP
30 Corporate Drive, Burlington, MA 01803

First published 2008

Notice
No responsibility is assumed by the publisher for any injury and/or damage to persons
or property as a matter of products liability, negligence or otherwise, or from any use
or operation of any methods, products, instructions or ideas contained in the material
herein.

British Library Cataloguing in Publication Data
A catalogue record for this book is available from the British Library

978 0 7506 8564 1

For information on all CIMA Publishing Publications
visit our website at www.cimapublishing.com

Typeset by Integra Software Services Pvt. Ltd, Pondicherry, India
www.integra-india.com

Printed and bound in Hungary
08 09 10 11 12   10 9 8 7 6 5 4 3 2 1

Contents

Introduction:
Not Another Book?

Where to, Maestro von Karajan?
You choose, I am in demand everywhere!

(1950s Viennese taxi joke)

Introduction

You are about to commence studies towards a professional accounting quali-fication. Ahead of you will be perhaps a couple of years (hopefully not many more!) of dedicated learning, which will need to be fitted in to all the other important calls on your time.

When these studies are over, you will join the ranks of many thousands of qualified accountants in the United Kingdom and very many more the world over. Accountancy is a well-respected career and, like the legal profession, it embraces a wide range of interesting work.

By choosing to commence your CIMA studies, you have chosen to go down a specialised path within the accountancy profession. This is the route which will eventually qualify you as a Chartered Management Accountant, with mem-bership of CIMA and the use of the designatory letters ACMA.

Students will come to these Managerial Level studies, with a wide variety of background education and preliminary qualifications, permitting them to take the CIMA exams at this level. The main Managerial Level entry routes are:

The CIMA Certificate in Business Accounting (CBA)
The Technician level exams of the AAT
Holding a "pure accountancy or business degree"
The Open University Certificate in Accounting
An MBA
Selected relevant professional qualifications

These entry options will, by their nature, have covered a range of syllabi and subjects. CIMA in 2006, reported that almost half of its graduate students have previously studied non-relevant degree subjects. A critical aspect of enrolling for the CIMA professional qualification, is therefore to ensure that you com-mence your studies at the right personal level.

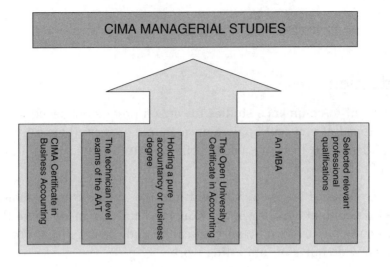

Like "Justice and the Ritz Hotel" (Lord Justice Matthew), the road to CIMA membership is open to all, regardless of educational background. CIMA has a flexible entry policy, that gives the opportunity to succeed. However, warns the Institute, you must be competent in mathematics and the English language before you start.

This is a KEY point, passed on to students from my practical teaching experience. DO ensure that you begin your studies where it best suits you. TAKE good advice and do not jump in beyond your capabilities. I have seen too many students do just that, then struggle, get disillusioned and either drop out or take much additional time and expense to qualify, "Hasten slowly, is the best approach"!

A strong recommendation in this respect, is to obtain the CIMA Certificate in Business Accounting, regardless of your other preliminary qualifications. It may take another 12 months towards your CIMA membership, but the five subjects studied there will provide a sound foundation towards the tougher Managerial Level studies.

Beyond the Managerial Level, lie the Strategic Level exams and then the TOPCIMA Case Study. The three Strategic Level Papers (P3, P6 and P9) are each 3-hour papers and all three have to be taken together at the first time of sitting. This is a formidable requirement, but as with the Managerial Level, students are awarded a permanent credit for any paper in which a candidate achieves a pass rate of 50% or more.

A very real problem that students have to face is that all of these examinations are time constrained. This in my experience, has come as a very nasty surprise, given some of the current assessment approaches used in universities and awarding bodies. So also is the lack of appreciation that failure rates are high and students must not expect to complete their qualification easily and within a short period of time.

The purpose of this book

Experience as a HE/FE College Lecturer at all levels in both Association of Accounting Technicians (AAT) and CIMA examinations since 1994, has increasingly shown a widening knowledge gap between the exam requirements of these two accountancy bodies. The author's polls in both 2005 and 2006, have conformed the difficulty that students have in studying for the Managerial Level. Soundings of those entering with relevant degrees, have supported this position.

This book, therefore, seeks to fill a preliminary knowledge gap in those areas which cause the greatest concern to those Managerial Level students who have not come up through the CIMA CBA route. It may also be useful, as refresher, to CBA students, as well as to students of financial administration generally.

In trying to meet the requirements of many different backgrounds, if there is a bias towards a particular type of student in this book, then it will be towards those who have come up via the AAT qualification. This route provides a significant number of entrants to Managerial Level studies and the syllabi that they have studied are both standardised and well publicised and are also supported by a range of specific training text books. My experience also confirms, that AAT students coming direct to this level of study, are those who are likely to find the going particularly tough.

In drafting the individual chapters, a course has tried to be steered between saying enough to give readers valuable preliminary knowledge and support, but not too much so as to duplicate the several study books available to them at Managerial Level.

Types of accountants in the United Kingdom

The UK professional accounting structure comprises six main bodies and three which provide important, specialist qualifications (the Chartered Institute of

Taxation, the Institute of Internal Auditors and the Association of Accounting Technicians). The six main bodies are the three Institutes of Chartered Accountants (England and Wales; Scotland; Northern Ireland), the Chartered Association of Certified Accountants (CACA) and the specialist public sector body (CIPFA).

Each of the bodies is long established and well respected. Leaving aside the specialist role of CIPFA in local government and the NHS, the "Chartereds" and the "Certifieds", traditionally specialise in financial accounting and reporting, both to the public and to corporate bodies, taxation and auditing.

That just leaves CIMA, which began life in 1919 as the Institute of Cost and Works Accountants (ICWA). In 1919, it became the Institute of Cost and Management Accountants (ICMA) and translated to its present title in 1995, on receipt of its Royal Charter. These changes are, in themselves, significant. "Cost and Works", being reminiscent of large engineering factories, translating raw materials into a wide range of metal goods, with much belching of smoke. As Chapter 1 of this book will show, modern business methods have moved on very significantly from the days of "make and store".

What do CIMA accountants do?

At this point in your career, you should hopefully have cleared your conscience that the Managerial Level studies are for you and have studied a copy of the latest edition of CIMA's "Qualification Structure and Syllabus". If so, you will know that it tells you all about the professional examination structure, taking you through the six papers at Managerial Level; three papers at Strategic Level and then on to TOPCIMA, the final test of professional competence.

A copy of that structure is included here, for ease of reference. From this, you will see the three Pillars, noting that each contains the word "management". The CIMA website is, of course, an invaluable source of information (www.cimaglobal.com). So also is an excellent CIMA publication entitled "Success in shaping your career". Both are compulsory reading, ladies and gentlemen! Appendix B at the back of this book contains a number of specific e-mail addresses for aspects of the work of CIMA's London headquarters.

CIMA is the only professional accountancy body that qualifies accountants solely for business. Its members work in industry and commerce and increasingly in the public sector, as that area of our economy becomes more concerned with value for money, competition and the bottom line.

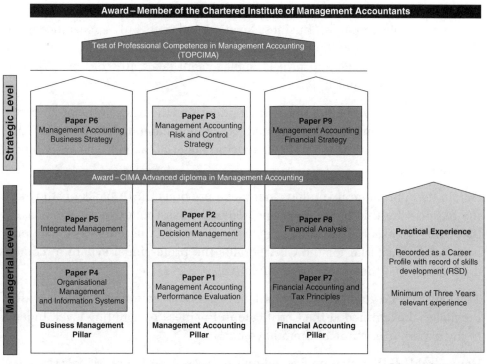

	Award – Member of the Chartered Institute of Management Accountants		

Test of Professional Competence in Management Accounting
(TOPCIMA)

Strategic Level

| Paper P6
Management Accounting
Business Strategy | Paper P3
Management Accounting
Risk and Control
Strategy | Paper P9
Management Accounting
Financial Strategy |

Award – CIMA Advanced diploma in Management Accounting

Managerial Level

| Paper P5
Integrated Management | Paper P2
Management Accounting
Decision Management | Paper P8
Financial Analysis | **Practical Experience**

Recorded as a Career
Profile with record of skills
development (RSD) |
| Paper P4
Organisational
Management
and Information Systems | Paper P1
Management Accounting
Performance Evaluation | Paper P7
Financial Accounting and
Tax Principles | Minimum of Three Years
relevant experience |
| **Business Management
Pillar** | **Management Accounting
Pillar** | **Financial Accounting
Pillar** | |

Pre-requisite Entry Requirement (e.g. CIMA Certificate in Business Accounting)

Prior experience can be included

The CIMA professional examination structure

The present scheme dates from 2005. The revision then was a "major update" and took place four years after the previous change – the business world is moving very quickly! The scheme shows that the Managerial Level requires success in six papers, two in each of the Learning Pillars. Completion of all six papers, awards the CIMA Advanced Diploma in Management Accounting.

The exam regulations permit these six papers to be taken in any order, but all six must be passed before moving on to the Strategic Level. Despite this, the Institute recommended that the papers should be attempted in the order 1, 4 and 7 before tackling 2, 5 and 8.

In the Management Accountant Pillar (broadly equivalent to a professionally focussed relevant degree), the P1 emphasis is on costing and budgeting principles and short-term decision making. Paper P2 looks at the implications of longer term decisions and cost planning. Papers P7 and P8 are the stuff of Chartered and Certified Accountants, where the emphasis is on producing financial reports which give a "true and fair view". P7 deals with a single entity and P8, with a group of companies. Business taxation makes its only appearance in the CIMA exams as 20% of the P7 syllabus. Managing human resources is a major component of Paper P4 and project management takes 40% of the studies on Integrated Management in P5.

There is a logicality in all of this, which underpins the basis of the professional examination scheme. This is that studies are incremental and cumulative and questions may be set which draw heavily on material taken from earlier blocks of study.

Herein lies a problem if you have not met a previous CIMA block of study and the reason why this book has been prepared. Classroom experience suggests that many Managerial Level candidates have not obtained the CBA. The published study material for the CBA heralds the professional syllabi to come – don't forget that the exams are cumulative!

Thus, there is no guarantee that all Managerial Level candidates have met all of the material examined at the Certificate in Business Accounting level. Indeed, in my experience, many of them have not.

Having said all that, you now stand on the threshold of your Managerial Level studies. To get you started therein, this bridging guide will concentrate on those five areas, where my teaching experience has highlighted a lack of confidence or knowledge. To quote many of my recent students, "there is a very large gap between our earlier studies and the Managerial Level".

I very much hope that this book will be of practical help in your early examination successes. With the CIMA qualification completed you will like the late, great Austrian conductor, Herbert von Karajan, be in demand everywhere!

Management
Accounting

I did the CIMA qualification and I'd take people from CIMA anytime
(Andrew Higginson)

Introduction

CIMA's *Official Terminology* in part defines management accounting as "the application of the principles of accounting and financial management to create, protect, preserve and increase value for the stakeholders of for-profit and not-for-profit enterprises in the public and private sectors. It is an integral part of management". The terminology defines financial accounting, as involving the recording of business transactions in accordance with the rules and their presentation in published statements at the end of an accounting period.

As we saw in the introduction, the main financial accounting bodies are the three Chartered Accountant Institutes and the CACA. CIMA and, to a lesser extent, CIPFA are really, on the basis of the definition above, the bodies for the promotion of management accounting.

In that chapter, we also saw how the name of CIMA had changed over the years, with its first title, including the words "cost" and "works", accurately reflecting the costing and pricing of factory production. In this chapter, we are going to look at both traditional and modern methods of management accounting, so we will start by seeing what you might have missed at CBA level.

Certificate in Business Accounting studies

Paper CO1 at CBA level is entitled the *Fundamentals of Management Accounting*. The basic syllabus comprises:

		%
A	Cost Determination	25
B	Cost Behaviour and Breakeven Analysis	10
C	Standard Costing and Variance Analysis	15
D	Costing and Accounting Systems	30
E	Financial Planning and Control	20

The basics of each of these syllabus areas will certainly have been studied at AAT Intermediate and Technician levels. Managerial Level Paper P1 further develops each of these areas and adds more advanced work on process costing (always a difficult area for students!), standard costing and budgeting. Paper P1, consistent with its title which incorporates *Performance Evaluation*, contains a 20% weighting relating to the use of management accounting principles in measuring areas of performance within a business. P1 is essentially concerned with the use of management accounting principles in short-term decision making, which are further developed in Paper P2. That paper also considers long-term decision making and, getting right up to date, how to use management accounting information to keep your business competitive.

Why Does Paper P1 Cause Problems?

Lecture room experience over many years has confirmed that this is so. Without exception, all classes of students starting their Managerial Level studies with P1, P4 and P7, find P4 the favourite followed by P7 and poor old P1 a long way behind! So why is it? I regularly asked them. The replies were pretty consistent and may be paraphrased thus:

- P4 – does not have many numbers, can be more easily related to the workplace and is more "waffly" than the other two;
- P7 – develops the principles of financial accounting which are already known and applies them to financial reporting in a single enterprise. If only there was not a big recent change from UK Standards to International Standards, life would be great! Most of what we do in this paper, has to be done to a set of rules and we need to know them;
- P1 – has more advanced standard costing, the awful process costing (both of which we don't like) and different people teach it or write it different ways, so we get confused.

Perhaps the initial answer to my earlier question lies in this last comment. Unlike financial accounting which is mainly set down in tablets of stone – the standards – management accounting has been built up on the basis of custom and practice, with very few stone tablets.

On reflection, it probably goes a little deeper than that and standard costing is an excellent example. In earlier management accounting studies, students were taught to crunch numbers in a certain way, without a deep appreciation of what the results meant. This was certainly a regular comment in Examiners Reports on each six monthly AAT exam diet. Not only may students meet a different way of crunching numbers in their CIMA studies but, even more so, they are now required to *think* about what the results mean and how they may be applied to the evaluation of business performance, or keeping ahead in a fast moving business environment. Another very good example of this knowledge shortfall concerns the interpretation of traditional performance measures – profitability, liquidity, efficiency, gearing and investor ratios.

It would be very unusual if a student came to study Paper P1, without meeting all or some of the topics which this chapter is going to examine. I have often met Managerial Level students with relevant degrees, who have little knowledge of standard costing and variance analysis and have not met process costing at all. This is relevant to answering the questions – What do I put in and in how much detail?

CBA Paper CO1

In an attempt to achieve this balance, I have looked at the detailed syllabus for the CBA Paper on *Fundamentals of Management Accounting* and used the sequential headings therein. Students who sat this paper, may therefore find this chapter useful as a refresher. It is to be hoped that all of the others will, as well. There will however, always be one!

Section E – Financial Planning and Control – is covered in the separate Chapter 5, Budgeting, of this book. Whilst these are very closely linked with many aspects of costing, particularly dealing with cost behaviour, the subject of budgeting is sufficiently important to merit a chapter all to itself.

The remaining syllabus Sections A–D, mentioned on page 3 will therefore be tackled in sequence and expanded as set out below. In place of E – Financial Planning and Control, the subject of Process Costing will be introduced in some detail. This subject gets no coverage at all in the CIMA CBA syllabus and only minimal coverage in AAT examinations.

A Cost Determination
   direct, indirect
   fixed, variable, hybrid (or semi-variable)
   absorption and marginal costing
   the Cost Statement
B Cost Behaviour
   fixed, variable and hybrid costs
   stepped costs
   analysing hybrid costs
   the concept of the contribution
   breakeven and CVP (cost–volume–profit) analysis

C   Standard Costing and Variance Analysis
      definition of standard costs
      benchmarking use
      calculation of standard costs
      variance analysis
      reconciliation statements
      interpretation of results
D   Process Costing
      definition of process costing
      dealing with questions
      losses and gains in process
      work in progress
      joint products and by-products
E   Cost Accounting Systems (Cost Bookkeeping)
      types of system
      ledger accounts preparation
      subjective and objective analysis
      coding systems

The chapter will conclude in Section F, with a questioning of these traditional approaches to management accounting and why new approaches are rapidly and significantly influencing many of the procedures summarised above.

A   Cost Determination

Introduction

You will recall from the introduction that CIMA's original name included the world "cost". Generations of accountancy students will have taken examination papers in "Costing". In essence, that word has now been translated into "Management Accounting". CIMA's *Official Terminology*, describes the word "cost" (as a verb), to ascertain the costs of a specified thing or activity. The word "cost" can rarely stand alone and should be qualified as to its nature and limitations.

There are many terms which include the word "cost" in the CIMA Terminology and most, if not all of them, will be included in this chapter. Two key, generic terms to introduce at this stage are:

1   Cost account – "a record of expenditure associated with a cost subject such as a job . . . "

2 Cost accounting – Gathering of costs information and its attachment to costs objects, the establishment of budgets, operations, processes, activities or products; and the analysis of variances, profitability or the social use of funds. The use of the term "costing" is not recommended except with a qualifying adjective, for example standard costing:

- batch costing
- continuous operation costing
- contract costing
- job costing
- service costing
- specific order costing
- marginal costing

The cost statement: direct and indirect costs

In theory (if not in practice), a business, building up the quoted cost of a future job, would prepare the following statement:

Direct costs
Labour	X
Materials	X
Other	X
Prime cost	X

Indirect costs
Production overheads	X
Factory cost	X
Administration overheads	X
Total cost	X

Allowance for profit
Mark up or margin	X
Selling price	X

Your local garage, if asked to quote for a big repair job on your car, would give you the selling price. The final invoice would probably just give a broad build up of the cost of materials used and so many hours of labour, at an hourly rate. Indirect costs and the profit allowance would be built in to the hourly labour rate.

Make sure that you are fully aware of the definitions of direct and indirect costs in preparing Cost Statements. Where you cannot ascribe particular expenditure to a specific job/customer, it will be treated as an indirect cost/overhead, coded to an overhead account and then recharged, pro rata, via a suitable overhead absorption rate (OAR) (overhead recovery rate, ORR), back to the job.

Fixed, variable and hybrid costs

As above, there are three basic terms here, with which you should be fully aware before you begin work on your P7 studies:

1. A *fixed cost* is that which tends, for an accounting period, to be unaffected by movements in a level of activity – e.g. output or turnover.
2. A *variable cost* is one which does vary as a level of activity changes.
3. A *hybrid cost* is a cost that is a mixture of a fixed element and a variable element. Hybrid costs need to be split into their fixed and variable elements and ways in which this might be done (e.g. scattergraph, high low) are exemplified in Chapter 5. This analysis is of particular importance in the preparation and flexing of budgets.

In this introduction to Management Accounting, there are two more important, basic terms to consider – absorption costing and marginal costing:

1. *Absorption costing* which codes all direct costs and all, or a proportion of overhead costs to a particular unit of output using a relevant OAR.
2. *Marginal costing* works on the basis that as fixed costs will be incurred anyway (subject to the definition above), decisions may be made without taking fixed costs into account. A marginal cost is therefore that variable cost that would be affected by the production, or non-production of an extra unit.

Outline Profit Statements prepared on each of these methods, would look as follows:

Absorption costing

Revenue		X
<u>Less</u>		
Variable Costs	(X)	
Fixed Costs	<u>(X)</u>	<u>(X)</u>
Profit		<u>X</u>

Marginal costing

Revenue	X
<u>Less</u>	
Variable Cost	(X)
Contribution	X
<u>Less</u>	
Fixed Cost	(X)
Profit	X

A key word here, which is examined later in this chapter, is "Contribution" (revenue less variable costs) reflecting the contribution that net revenue makes firstly, to meeting fixed costs, with the remainder forming the profit.

To ensure confidence in calculating OARs, look at the full and detailed exercise and model answer below – there is also revision question on the same theme, at the end of this chapter.

Calculating Overhead Absorption Rates

In looking at the build-up of a cost statement earlier in this chapter, we saw that expenses which can be directly allocated to a job, are coded straight thereto. This will typically be labour, materials and any other expenditure (e.g. a special piece of equipment) which has been specifically incurred. Added together, these direct costs form the prime cost of a job.

Any business, however, will incur costs which cannot be allocated to a specific task. Heating, lighting, business rates, postage, etc. are some examples of indirect costs or overheads. They may relate to the production process (production overheads) or to the supporting office administration. These costs have to be recovered from customers and this done through the calculation of an OAR, otherwise called an ORR (Overhead Recovery Rate).

Typically, overheads will be absorbed into a job through an OAR per labour or machine hour; per unit of production, or as a % of labour or prime cost. The "3As" procedure is therefore:

1. Allocate direct costs straight to the the job or cost centre.
2. Apportion overheads from an overheads account to the relevant cost centre.
3. Absorb overheads into a job from the relevant cost centre, via an OAR.

Let us now look further at Step 2-apportionment. A company makes a product which passes through three manufacturing processes, or stages, each located in a separate building. How much of the total business rates bill for the whole factory, relates to each process/building? This might be done by apportioning the total rates bill, pro rata, to space occupied, since size is a key ingredient in determining the size of the total bill. The total cost of heating and lighting might be apportioned to each cost centre according to space occupied, or hours worked in each building. Telephone costs might be apportioned pro rata to the number of extensions in each cost centre and supervisory salaries could be shared out on the basis of time spent in each cost centre, from a time sheet analysis.

Overheads are thus apportioned to cost centres on the PRATSOO basis – Pro RAta To Something Or Other. and in an examination question requiring the calculation of an OAR, there will be a number of bases for YOU to select a most appropriate one having regard to the nature of the expense. Different students may select different bases and get different answers as a result . . . all correct in principle!

Example 1

A company has three production cost centres; machining, assembly and finishing and these are supported by two service departments called stores and canteen. The budgeted expenditure for next year is £982,900 analysed as follows:

	Direct labour	Materials	Other expenditure
M	340,800	165,000	16,400
A	130,000	103,000	19,600
F	65,000	37,000	8,550
S	10,000	5,900	31,450
C	14,200	Nil	36,000
	560,000	310,900	112,000

From past experience, it is calculated that the costs of the two service departments support the production process in the following % proportions:

	M	A	F	S
Stores	55	35	10	0
Canteen	45	35	10	10

Notice how the stores benefits from the use of the canteen, but that there is no reciprocal arrangement.

All of these costs may now be placed into an overhead analysis matrix:

Cost	M	A	F	S	C	Total
Labour	340,800	130,000	65,000			535,800
Materials	165,000	103,000	37,000			305,000
Labour overhead				10,000	14,200	24,200
Material overhead				5,900		5,900
Other overhead	16,400	19,600	8,550	31,450	36,000	112,000
Total	522,200	252,600	110,550	47,350	50,200	982,900

At this stage, all of the budgeted costs have been allocated to the five cost centres. Since the S and C costs are not directly related to the manufacture of goods that are then sold, these costs must be reapportioned to the three production cost centres that earn an honest crust. The PRATSOO for this stage has been given in the table of percentages and once this has been done, all of our budgeted costs have either been allocated or apportioned to the three centres of production:

Cost	M	A	F	S	C	Total
Direct costs (above)	505,800	233,000	102,000			840,800
Overhead (above)	16,400	19,600	8,550	47,350	50,200	142,100
Canteen	22,590	17,570	5,020	5,020	(50,200)	0
Total	38,990	37,170	13,570	52,370	0	142,100
Stores	28,803	18,330	5,237	(52,370)	0	0
Totals	67,793	55,500	18,807	0	0	142,100
Budget total	573,593	288,500	120,807	0	0	982,900

The overheads totalling £142,100 have now been apportioned to the production cost centres and the final task now, is to calculate the OAR for each of the production cost centres.

In this company, the M shop absorbs overheads on the basis of machine hours, but as A and F are essentially manual tasks, they absorb on the basis of labour hours.

The budgeted hours for each shop for next year are

Machine	27,118 hours
Assembly	5,045 hours
Finishing	1,447 hours

Giving the following OAR for each productive cost centre:

Machine	£67,793/27,118 = £2.50 per machine hour
Assembly	£55,500/5,045 = £11.00 per labour hour
Finishing	£18,807/1,447 = £13.00 per labour hour

This means that if a job passes through all three production shops, taking 8 hours in M; 5 hours in A and 3 hours in F, it would absorb total overheads of £114.00, as follows:

M 8 × £2.50	= 20.00
A 5 × £11.00	= 55.00
F 3 × £13.00	= 39.00
Total	£114.00

And, when added to the direct costs of the job, would form the total cost, to which the profit element would be added before billing the customer.

Under/over absorption

The basic figures which were used in this example – the sums of money and the hours were all budgeted. The resultant OARs would need careful and regular monitoring during the year and adjusted as circumstances dictate, to ensure that there is no significant under recovery (a charge against profit) or over recovered (when goods may be overpriced and therefore not competitive).

Activity-based recovery rates

Our example also made references to the mnemonic PRATSOO. This is not an official term, but it may be an useful aide-mémoire to the reader. Elsewhere in this book, our Harvard academics, Kaplan and Norton, make several appearances. In connection with the calculation of OARs, they were instrumental in offering a new approach. Their book, *The Fall and Rise of Management Accounting* (1987), suggested that the build up of product costs on the "hit and miss" PRATSOO basis, was not acceptable for a profession which prided itself on accuracy. Instead Kaplan and Norton proposed that overheads should be apportioned on the basis of the activities which caused them in the first place. Thus was born ABC or activity-based costing.

In our example, the stores costs were £52,370. These were apportioned to the costs of production on the basis of broad percentages, built up from "past experience" – whose? when? ABC requires that we ask what are the stores there for and what causes or *drives* those costs? The stores must be there to provide the goods when required for production. The more requests (requisitions/issue notes) that are made, will drive the stores overhead upwards. If we assume that in the period covered by our example, requisitions made were from M 7500; A 2100: F 1000, then the apportioned overheads would have been, respectively, £37,055: £10,375 and F £4940.

Based, therefore on the activities which caused the stores costs, the machine shop was under apportioned by £8252; the assembly shop was £7955 over apportioned and the finishing shop would have received about £300 less. Such differences are significant (material) in a profession with a primary task of accurate recording and price calculation.

Under ABC, the Stores cost centre totalling £52,370, would be designated a "cost pool" and activities which caused these costs (requisitions or issue notes) would be called "cost drivers". Thus, with a total of 10,600 requisitions, the cost driver rate would have been £52,370/10,600 = £4.94 per issue.

B Cost Behaviour and Breakeven Analysis

CIMA defines Cost Behaviour as the "variability of input costs with activity undertaken. Cost may increase proportionately with increasing activity (the usual assumption for a variable cost), or it may not change with increased activity (a fixed cost). Some costs (semi-variable) may have both variable and fixed elements. Other behaviour is possible, costs may increase more or less than in direct proportion, and there may be step changes in cost, for example. To a large extent cost behaviour will be dependent on the timescale assumed".

Cost behaviour, apart from being defined in Section A of this chapter, may also be depicted both as aggregate costs and costs per unit graphically, as follows:

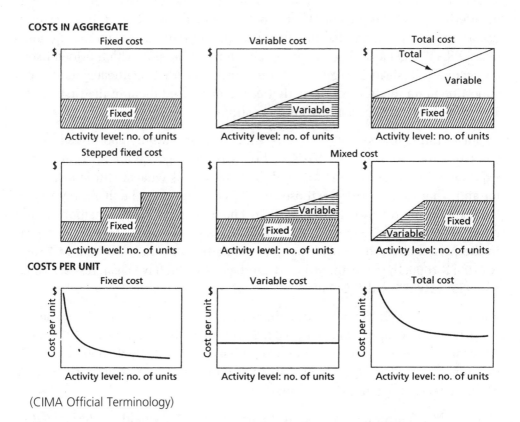

(CIMA Official Terminology)

Note particularly, the stepped fixed cost (where e.g. production requirements need an additional building which increases business rates) and the way in which fixed costs, when spread over a greater number of production units, causes total cost to decline.

The *contribution* is an important term in Marginal Costing and its place in the make-up of a Marginal Cost Statement and its definition given earlier, should be well known. Contribution may be expressed in total, per unit, or as a percentage of sales.

One further aspect of Cost Behaviour needs to be looked at before we move on, since will meet more of Breakeven Analysis in your P1 studies.

Breakeven analysis often and more correctly called cost–volume–profit (CVP) analysis, considers the relationship between costs, volume and profit at different levels of activity. This enables the calculation of the breakeven point (at which there is neither profit nor loss), the contribution/sales (C/S) ratio and the margin of safety (MOS). Let us look at each of these in turn:

(i) The *breakeven point* is where there are sufficient contributions to exactly meet fixed costs. You can usually calculate this arithmetically before drawing a graph, if one is asked for. Thus, if fixed costs are £63,000; the variable cost is £15 per unit and expected sales are 10,000 units @ £24 each:

> The unit contribution is £9 and 7000 contributions will be needed to meet the total of fixed cost. Breakeven is therefore achieved at 7000 units and, when all units are sold, the total profit is £27,000. Each unit above 7000 sold contributes £9 to profit, but there is a loss of £90 if only 6990 are sold.

This may be expressed graphically, as follows, on a breakeven chart:

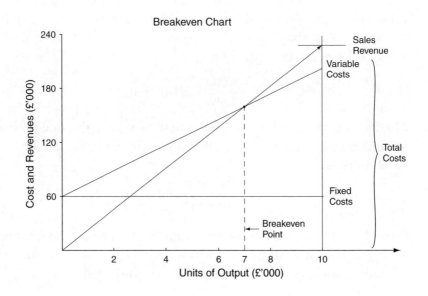

23

This scenario may also be expressed in the form of a *profit/volume chart*, as follows

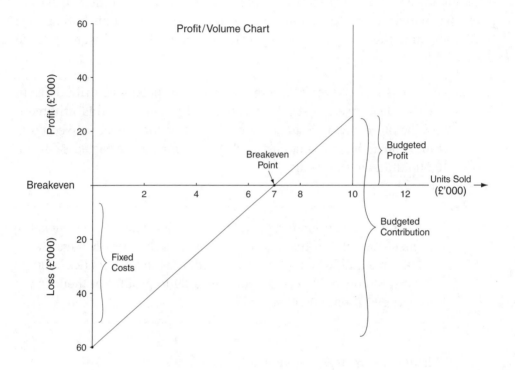

(ii) The *C/S ratio* is a measure of the size of the contribution gained from each £1 of sales. In the above example, the ratio is $^C/_S$ or $^9/_{24}$ a ratio of 37.5%. With fixed costs of £63,000, breakeven occurs at the point where sales revenue is equal to:

$$\frac{63,000}{37.5\%} = £168,000$$

(iii) Finally, the MOS calculates the extent to which the budgeted sales volume may fall before moving into a loss. In our example, the MOS is 3000 units, or

$$\frac{3000}{10,000} = 30\%$$

Having looked briefly at some of the important basics of the cost accounting, all of which you will meet in more detail in your P1 studies, it is time to get down to what teaching experience tells me are the BIG problem areas!

Students have traditionally always had difficulties with *standard costing and variance analysis* (SCVA). The bad news, is that the basic themes of SCVA, which you may already have met, have more advanced variations thereon in the P1 Paper! The good news, which we will meet at the end of this chapter, is that traditional standard costing is under criticism and change and the P1 candidates in 2017 may well not have to learn what you now need to go through!

An even nastier aspect of cost accounting is *Process Costing*: It may not appear to loom large in the totality of the P1 syllabus, but it is there all the same, so the principles need to be addressed.

Finally, we will look at two types of *Cost Accounting (Bookkeeping) Systems* – Firstly, under traditional costing methods and then, those which reflect current changes in those methods.

C   Standard Costing and Variance Analysis

In essence, standard costing is an aspect, or technique, of budgetary control, which firstly establishes what a job should cost and then investigates material differences between the standard cost and the actual cost. It is of particular value where the output is routine and the cost element may be easily measured.

In building up the standard cost of a job, it is essential to use up to date figures and then keep unit costs up to movements in the market. After all, you would not quote current prices to a customer for a job to be undertaken in 3 months time, knowing that there was a significant national pay rise in the interim.

There are two important definitions in the CIMA *Official Terminology*:

A standard is a benchmark measurement of resource usage or revenue or profit generation, set in defined conditions

A standard cost is a planned unit cost of a produce, component or service, which may be determined on a number of bases. Two particular bases are, firstly, that which is set before activity commences (ex ante) and secondly that which is set after the event (ex post). In the latter case, it can represent the optimum achievable level of performance in the conditions which were actually experienced

---

A typical SCVA exercise in the Management Accounting Fundamentals papers of the CBA is to compare the standard cost of producing a single unit of a product with the actual cost and then examine (analyse) the differences (variances). All this, is to find out why there were differences and, if necessary, adjust the standard costs for future business use. It would be usual also, for there to be revenues, as well as costs involved in an exercise, in which case we will need to examine the reasons for differences between expected profit and actual profit.

We are now going to work through a complete SCVA exercise at CBA level, to prepare you for a more advanced look at this technique in your P1 Studies:

Example 2

The standard cost card per unit of a "Wiggy" shows:

Materials	6 kg A @ £3/kg	18.00	
	3 kg B @ £9/kg	27.00	45.00
Labour	4 hours @ £6/hour		24.00
		Prime Cost	69.00
Variable overheads	4 hours @ £2/hour		8.00
			£77.00*
Fixed overheads	4 hours @ £1.50/hour		6.00
	Standard Cost per Unit		£83.00**

         * Total cost under marginal costing

       ** Total cost under absorption costing

The factory where "Wiggys" are made, uses total absorption costing
In month 6 of the financial year, it was budgeted to make and sell 1000 "Wiggys" @ £120 each

The actual costs per unit, were as follows:

Materials	5 kg A	@ £4/kg
	3 kg B	@ £9/kg
Labour	4½ hours @ £5.00	

Variable overheads – the actual hourly rate was £1.80
Fixed overheads – the actual hourly rate was £1.60

Actual sales were 980 @ £118 per unit

What can be generally established from this?

Materials – cost more than expected, but we used less, in total

Labour – took fewer hours, but each hour costs more

Variable and fixed overheads – You will see that these are absorbed into the total cost of the product at so much per hour of labour. Not only did the number of labour hours per unit increase, but the hourly rate of each type of overhead also changed

Selling price – Both actual revenue per unit and total units sold were below budgeted expectations

The standard cost of a unit was calculated at £83.00. The actual cost was £84.80, made up as follows:

Materials	A	20.00	
	B	27.00	47.00
Labour			22.50
Variable overhead		8.10	69.50
Fixed overhead		7.20	15.30
			£84.80

The total cost variance, was therefore £1.80 per unit worse than expected. In the language of SCVA, this is an *adverse variance* (written as ADV, or just (A)). If it had been better than the standard, the designation would have been *favourable* (FAV, or (F)).

As 1000 "Wiggys" were made, the overall ADV variance was:

1,000 × Standard cost of 83.00	83,000	
1,000 × Actual cost of 84.80	84,800	
Total variance	£1,800	(A)

And we would reconcile the standard cost to the actual cost by preparing the following statement, analysing each total variance over its subvariances:

Standard cost			£83,000	
Materials – quantity		Individual unit		1,000 units
A	1 kg @ £3	3.00		3,000 (F)
B	3 kg @ £9	–		–
			3.00	
Materials – price				
A	5 kg @ £1	5.00		5,000 (A)
B	3 kg @ £9	–		–
			5.00	
Labour – quantity				
½ hour @ £6		3.00		3,000 (A)
4½ hours @ £1		4.50	7.50	4,500 (F)
Variable overheads – quantity				
½ hour @ £2		1.00		1,000 (A)
Variable overheads – price				
4½ hours @ 20p		0.90	1.90	900 (F)
Fixed overheads – quantity				
½ hour @ £1.50/hour		0.75		750 (A)
Fixed overheads – Price				
4½ hours @ 10p/hour		0.45		450 (A)
Actual cost			£84,800	1,800 (A)

If we now bring revenue into the reckoning, the sales variance may be calculated as:

Standard revenue	1,000 units @ £120	£120,000
(what was expected)		
Actual revenue	980 units @ £118	£115,000
		£4,360 (A)

Here, both the *quantity* sold and the *price* per unit, were below what was expected – a double dose of Adverse news:

Quantity variance	20 units @ £120	2400
Price variance	980 units @ £2	1960
		4360

A reconciliation between expected and actual profit for "Wiggys" in Month 6 would therefore be:

Expected (budgeted) profit:

Revenue		120,000
Cost		83,000
Budgeted profit		37,000
Sales variance		4,460 (A)
Revised profit		32,640
Cost variances		
Materials	2,000 (A)	
Labour	1,500 (F)	
Variable Overheads	100 (A)	
Fixed Overheads	1,200 (A)	1,800 (A)
Actual profit		£30,840

Looking at all of these calculations in more detail, we can see that the total variance of £1800 (A) has occurred because the actual cost of a unit was greater than the expected (standard) cost. Within that total variance, the cost of labour was better than expected, but the other three cost elements were all worse than planned.

Notice also that each of the cost variances is due either to the actual price or the actual quantity being different from the standard. Looking at each element in turn, the quantity of material A used, was 1 kg less than expected. At a standard price of £3 per kg and with 1000 units made, that gives a favourable quantity variance of £3000:

$$1\,kg \times £3 \times 1000$$

Material B's quantity used was exactly as per the standard, thus giving a nil variance.

The price of material A was, however, £1 per kg greater than expected and we used 5 kg giving a total material A price variance of:

$$5\,kg \times £1 \times 1000 = £5000 \,(A)$$

Again, material B was exactly as expected.

The same principles apply to each of the three other cost elements and also to the sales revenue.

Each cost element has a variance for a change in price (P), or a change in quantity (Q) and follows the formula:

Price variance   − difference in price   × quantity used/ sold
Quantity variance − difference in quantity × standard cost

It is clear from our example, that both the variable and fixed overheads are absorbed into the standard cost of a unit on the basis of so much per labour hour. The labour hours, expected to be 4 per unit, turned out to be an extra half hour.

As the quantity of labour increased, so did the amount of overhead absorbed. Some good news was that the actual hourly rate for variable overheads dropped, from a standard £2 to £1.80 actual, saving $4\frac{1}{2}$ hours @ 20p per hour. The rate for fixed overheads, however, was 10p higher, resulting in an additional actual cost per unit of 45p and £450 for all 1000 "Wiggys" made.

All variances are therefore either P or Q though, in practice, they go by different names, as this table shows:

Element	P sub variance	Q sub variance
Material	Price	Usage
Labour	Rate	Efficiency
Variable Overhead	Expenditure	Efficiency
Fixed Overhead	Expenditure	Volume
Sales	Price	Quantity

"Every time things are going well, you've forgotten something!" This old adage, a variation on Sod's law, raises itself in variance analysis at this study level. It concerns the variance for fixed overheads. Our table above shows that the price variance is termed "expenditure" and the quantity variance is called "volume". In practice (i.e. the examination room!) you may well be required to split the fixed overheads volume variance into two more, entitled capacity and efficiency.

This arises because the annual quantity of fixed overheads is calculated before the year commences. The budget for fixed overheads is assumed, by its nature, to be a fixed sum, whereas that for variable overheads will change during the year and the absorption rate will be regularly reviewed. In a typical examination question, the budgeted production quantity for a particular period will be different in practice. In addition the budgeted expenditure itself may change. The example below, brings all of these fixed overheads implications together.

Example 3

Colin plc manufactures a "Vikkas". It is November and the budget for the following year beginning on 1 January, has been prepared. It is planned to manufacture 144,000 Vikkas, 12,000 in each month of the year. Fixed overheads are budgeted at £576,000 and each Vikka takes 4 labour hours to manufacture

We now fast forward to the actuals for the year. Demand was higher than estimated and 13,000 a month were made. Because of this, a factory extension was necessary and additional business rates of £20,000 made the actual fixed overheads £596,000

Total labour hours worked were 618,000

The task requires the calculation of the fixed overheads total variance, of the two sub variances and the two sub—sub variances.

Given the initial budget information, it can be calculated that the budgeted fixed overheads absorption rate was £4 per unit and thus £1 per labour hour. Over the year, an extra 12,000 Vikkas were made and 156,000 units should have taken 624,000 labour hours: they took 6000 labour hours fewer. The required variances are as follows:

		Total	
Incurred		596,000	
Absorbed		624,000	
Total		28,000	(F)

Expenditure		*Volume*		
Budget	576,000	Budget	$144,000 \times £4 =$	576,000
Actual	596,000	Standard	$156,000 \times 4 =$	624,000
	£20,000 (A)			£48,000 (F)

Capacity (hours $\times$ £1)			Efficiency		
Budget	576,000	Standard	$624,000 \times £1$	624,000
Actual	618,000	Actual	$618,000 \times £1$	618,000
	£42,000 (F)			£6,000 (F)

Important comments on the answer calculations are as follows:

Notice how the P and Q sub variances equal the total variance and the sub–sub variances for capacity and efficiency equal that for volume. Thus, variance calculations are always checkable!

The total variance was favourable because we made and sold an extra 12,000 units, each one bringing in an *unbudgeted* £4 per unit. This additional £48,000 (shown in the volume sub variance) was offset by an additional expenditure on fixed overheads of £20,000.

Capacity and efficiency variances are traditionally calculated in hours (either labour or machine), multiplied by the rate per hour.

The Capacity sub variance is favourable, because Colin has the capacity to produce more for paying customers – always good for a business! The Efficiency sub variance is also favourable, because the workforce saved 6000 hours.

The term "standard" is used in the volume variance because that was what was to be done.

That completes the basic work on SCVA. There will be an additional "full" exercise to be attempted, on page 39 of this chapter. It is important to have plenty of practice in these basic calculations, as the standard costing work in Paper P1 will build on these principles. Be prepared to offer reasons why variances might have occurred, keeping these simple (e.g. the labour efficiency rate was (F), because the most highly qualified workforce was employed on that task. Since they merited a higher rate of pay than the standard workforce, the labour rate variance was (A)).

Since fixed overhead variances always seem to cause the most trouble to students, get to know the structure of the calculations shown in the example above. Employ the line "*B*ruce *S*pringsteen flies *B*ritish *A*irways to *S*outh *A*frica", for the order of the ingredients in Volume, Capacity and Efficiency (not forgetting that C comes before E!).

D   Process Costing

Earlier in this chapter, Process Costing was referred to as an "even nastier aspect of cost accounting". As with standard costing, many students feel very uncomfortable when dealing with process costing questions, so as with standard costing, we will concentrate on the basics which will be developed and potentially examined in your P1 studies.

CIMA's *Official Terminology* defines process costing as a "form of costing applicable to continuous processes where process costs are attributed to the number of units produced. This may involve estimating the number of equivalent units (EU) in stock at the start and end of the period under consideration".

The main feature of process costing is that the end product passes through a series of sequential stages, or processes, from raw material to finished goods, with the output of each stage forming the input to the next, until the final output appears in the final process. On the way, there may be expected and unexpected losses, but there may also be waste (which can be a saleable by-product), or a stage may be reached where instead of one final product, two or more (joint) products may appear, or be capable of being developed separately in further processes.

Because the process is continuous, and labour material and overhead costs are added at each stage, it is not possible to build up unit costs of output or closing stock. As we are dealing with a single homogeneous mass, problems arise in the valuation of opening and closing work in progress. In addition, individual elements of conversion cost may not be added in equal proportions and these proportions need to be taken into account in valuations.

Two other unique features of process costing need to be mentioned, before moving into a practical example:

- The concept of the "EU" and
- The layout of process accounts which have a Dr and Cr column for both quantity and money, as in the following example:

Process 1 account

	Units	£		Units	£
Materials	7,000	120,000	Output to Process 2	7,000	210,000
Labour		60,000			
Overhead		30,000			
	7,000	210,000		7,000	210,000

Process 2 account

	Units	£		Units	£
From Process 1	7,000	210,000			
More materials	1,500	55,000	Completed output to Finished goods A/C	8,500	310,000
More labour		22,000			
More overhead		23,000			
	8,500	310,000		8,500	310,000

This is a very untypical example, as there are no losses (either expected or unexpected) and no messy equivalent units. It shows how the output of Process 1 flows naturally to the final stage, where more "conversion costs" are added. The whole output is now available for sale and the cost of making each unit has been £310,000/8500 = £36.47.

If only the examination room could be as simple!

We will shortly to work through complete example (4), which will involve most, if not all, of the particular terminology, associated with process costing. Before we start, here are the CIMA *Official Terminology* definitions:

Normal loss	Expected loss, allowed for in the budget, and normally calculated as a percentage of the good output from a process during a period of time. Normal losses are generally either valued at zero or at their disposal values
Abnormal loss	Any loss in excess of the normal loss allowance. It is isolated as a period entry rather than as a component of product cost
Abnormal gain	Improvement on the accepted or normal level of loss associated with a production activity. It is isolated as a period entry rather than as an adjustment to product cost
Equivalent units	Notional whole units representing uncompleted work. Used to apportion costs between work in progress and completed output, and in performance assessment

Scrap	Discarded material having some value
Cost, weighted average	Method of unit cost determination, often applied to stocks, in which an average unit cost is calculated, when a new purchase quantity is received
By-product	Output of some value produced incidentally while manufacturing the main product
Joint products	Two or more products produced by the same process and separated in processing, each having a sufficiently high saleable value to merit recognition as a main product.

Losses in production

The simple example of Process accounts that has just been shown, had no losses in production. In practice, as the *Official Terminology* definitions show, we will expect to meet normal and abnormal losses.

Normal losses are those that are expected and its extent is based on experience, say 10% of input:

	£
Input materials 2,000 kg cost	15,000
Labour and overheads	12,000
Normal loss	10%
Actual output	1,800 kg

Here you would expect to lose 10% of 2000 kg = 200 kg and that is exactly what has happened.

The Process account will show:

	kg	£		kg	£
Material	2,000	15,000	Normal loss	200	–
Labour and overheads		12,000	Output	1,800	27,000
	2,000	27,000		2,000	27,000

Both sides balance and the cost per kg is £15.00.

If that normal loss can be sold as scrap (at £5 per kg), the proceeds are credited to the Process account and the production cost per unit falls to £14.44 per kg.

	kg	£		kg	£
Material	2,000	15,000	Normal loss	200	1,000
Labour and overheads		12,000	Output	1,800	26,000
	2,000	27,000		2,000	27,000

Scrap account

	kg	£		kg	£
Process account	200	1000	Cash/bank	200	1000

If the expected loss was greater than 200 kg, then we have an *Abnormal loss*, which will finish up as an expense and reduce profits: assuming that the actual loss in our example was 250 kg, the accounts will appear as follows:

Process account

	kg	£		kg	£
As before	2,000	27,000	Normal loss	200	1,000
			Abnormal loss	50	722
			Output	1,750	25,278
	2,000	27,000		2,000	27,000

Both types of loss are sold at £5 per kg and the Abnormal loss is valued as part of the remaining cost per unit – i.e. £26,000÷1800 = £14.44.

Scrap account

	kg	£		kg	£
Process account			Cash/bank	250	1,250
Normal loss	200	1,000			
Abnormal					
Loss account	50	250			
	250	1,250		250	1,250

Abnormal loss account

	kg	£		kg	£
Process account	50	722	Scrap account	50	250
			Profit and loss		
			Account		472
	50	722		50	722

An *Abnormal gain* is created when the actual loss experienced is less than the anticipated Normal loss. Assuming that the actual loss in our example was 150, then there is an Abnormal gain of 50 kg and our Process account will show:

Process account

	kg	£		kg	£
As before	2,000	27,000			
			Normal loss	200	1,000
Abnormal gain account	50	722	Output	1,850	26,722
	2,050	27,722		2,050	27,722

The Abnormal gain account will then be credited and that account cleared by a debit, which will be credited to the Profit and Loss Account.

A key feature of process costing, mentioned earlier, is the concept of EU. The examples so far, have assumed that all units are completed at the end of an account period, but that may not be so:

If production costs in a month are £27,000 and if, at the end of that period, there are 600 units fully completed and 300 completed to the extent of 80%, then the equivalent units are 600+ (80% of 300) = 840, the cost per equivalent unit is £27,000÷840 =£32.143 and the value of that period's production is:

	Units	£
Finished	600	19,286
Work in progress	240	7,714
	840	£27,000

A further variation on the theme of EU is that it is very unlikely that all incomplete units are exactly 80% complete. There may be different proportions of incompleteness for labour and for materials, so each element of input will need a separate calculation of equivalent units. To follow our example through, on the basis that materials are totally input, but labour is only one-third complete:

	Materials			Labour	
		% Complete	EU	% Complete	EU
Started and completed	800	1	800	1	800
In progress	300	1	300	$^1/_3$	100
	1,100		1,100		900
Cost per EU (£)		15,000		12,000	
		1,100	=13.6363	900	=13.3333
Cost of finished production	800× 13.6363		=10,909	800 × 13.3333	=10,666
Cost of work in progress	300× 13.6363		=4,091	100 × 13.3333	=1,334
			£15,000		£12,000

The examples just considered have made the assumption that there was no opening stock of work in progress or subsequent changes. There are two methods of accounting for stock movements. At the CBA level, only the weighted average cost method is examinable but at the Managerial Level you will also meet the FIFO method.

The averaging method simply adds opening stock values to current conversion costs to provide an overall average cost per EU this is shown in Example 3.

Example 4

Work in progress at 1 March, 30,000 units, 40% complete. During March, 60,000 units were started and 80,000 were completed in that month. During the month, added costs were £49,500 for materials and £40,000 other. Work in progress at 1 March was valued at £20,500 (Materials £18,000, Other £2500)

The task is to calculate finished production values for March and work in progress at 31 March using the averaging method

Flows of unit
Work in progress
at 1 March   30,000
Add in month   60,000
                              90,000
Less completed   80,000

Work in progress
at 31 March   10,000

EU calculation

	Materials	Other
Completed	80,000	80,000
Work in progress (50% complete)	10,000	5,000
	90,000	85,000

Relevant Costs

	Materials	Other	Total
Work in progress at 1 March	18,000	2,500	20,500
Added in month	49,500	4,000	89,500
	£67,500	£42,500	£110,000
Cost per EU	75p	50p	
Cost of completed work	$80,000 \times 75p = 60,000$	$80,000 \times 50p = 40,000$	100,000
Cost of work in progress	$10,000 \times 75p = 7,500$	$5,000 \times 50p = 2,500$	10,000
	£67,500	£42,500	£110,000

Process account

	Units			Units	
Work in progress @ 1 March	30,000	20,500	Output	80,000	100,000
Added in month	60,000	89,500	Work in progress @ 31 March	10,000	10,000
	90,000	£110,000		90,000	£110,000

With the valuation of stock on the FIFO method, the total output is divided between opening work in progress and units started/completed in the period. The cost of the opening work in progress is NOT added to costs incurred in the period, but instead is valued on an equivalent units basis.

Reference was made at the beginning of this section on process costing to *by-products* and *joint products*, and CIMA definitions of these terms given.

The proceeds from the casual sale of by-products is either credited directly to the Profit and loss account, or to the Process account, reducing the unit cost of production.

Joint products are those with a greater financial return to the business and are reached at a certain point of production where, from the "homogeneous mass" then existing, separate saleable products may be created either immediately or after some further conversion. The question is, how are pre separation costs for each joint product arrived at? This may be done either by physical measurement, or by potential proportions of market sales value based on experience.

E   Cost Accounting Systems (Cost Bookkeeping)

CIMA's *Official Terminology* introduces you to two methods of cost bookkeeping:

1   Integrated accounts – a set of accounting records that integrate both financial and cost accounts, using a common input of data for all accounting purposes . . .
2   Interlocking accounts – a set of accounting records where the cost and financial accounts are distinct, the two being kept continuously in agreement by the use of control accounts or reconciled by other means . . .

Since integrated accounts use just one set of records to serve both cost accounting and financial accounting and the CBA syllabus is based thereon, our initial example will also be based thereon.

Before so doing, look back to earlier in this chapter and to the make up of a job cost sheet. Materials are brought in, worked on by labour, manufacturing and administrative overheads are added to give a total cost of production and, finally, a profit allowance gives the selling price.

Consider the movement of all this through a factory. Raw materials become completed goods which are then sold. Thus, there are three different types of stock at different stages of production (raw materials: work in progress and finished goods). The Manufacturing and Profit and loss account brings all these transactions together to show a period's good or bad news. At all stages, cash, debtors and creditors accounts are involved.

Integrated accounts work in a way that reflects this "flow". Which T accounts are involved and how they link together, are depicted below:

Raw materials control

• Buy raw materials and put into stock A	• Take out of stock to work on B • Closing stock

Labour (Wages) control account

• Wages paid over E • Tax paid over F	• Wages due (workforce) C • Wages due (Production overhead) D

Administration overhead account

• Administration costs paid G	• Costs to profit and Loss account H

Production overhead account

• Production costs paid D	• Work in progress account (overheads absorbed) J • Balance (costs not yet absorbed)

Work in progress account

• Wages due* C • Raw materials used B • Production overhead Absorbed* J	• Transfer to finished Goods account K

(* Production overheads absorbed at X% of direct wages costs)

Creditors account

• Bank account payments Q	• Raw materials and other creditors A

PAYE Creditor's account

• Bank – tax paid R • Balance	• Wages control – tax due F

Debtors account

• Sales N	• Bank – cash received P
	• Balance

Sales account

• Profit and loss account O	• Debtors account N

Bank account

• Debtors P	• Cheque payments E, F, G, Q, R

Cost of sales account

• Finished goods L	• Profit and loss M

Profit and loss account

• Cost of sales M	• Sales O
• Administration –overheads H	
• Net profit	

Question 7 at the end of this chapter contains an example of integrated accounting bookkeeping based on standard costs.

Two small, but important, syllabus inclusions now complete this section. The syllabus speaks of subjective and objective analysis and also of coding systems. These terms are linked together on page 8 of CIMA's *Official Terminology* as follows:

Code   Brief, accurate reference designed to assist classification of items by facilitating entry, collation and analysis. For example, in costing, the first three digits in the code 211,392 might indicate the nature of the expenditure (*subjective classification*), and the last three digits might indicate the cost centre or cost unit to be charged (*objective classification*).

For example, the code 2/1/1/39/1 might breakdown as follows:

2/	Salary payment
1/1	High Street Wigan Branch for the month of January
39/	Soft furnishings department
1	Capital expenditure

Subjective aspects of the code relate to the nature of the expenditure (in this case a January *salary* payment) while 391 represents the proposal (in this case, a major *extension* to part of the Wigan Branch). Code lists are, by their nature, capable of great flexibility and can provide for an infinite degree of cost, or revenue, analysis.

F The Changing Face of Management Accounting

A major new aspect of Management Accounting, which will be met in Paper P1 concerns the impact on traditional methods of the modern business environment. The move is one away from "make and stock", to more flexible manufacturing systems based on making what the customer requires, when it is wanted. "Just in Time (JIT)" systems aim to produce or procure products or components as required. This applies to the purchasing of materials, as well as to a "pull" system, where production is determined by demand, instead of a "push" system where full production regardless, may result in expensive overstocking of products.

Modern systems rely significantly upon the Japanese "kaizen" principle of continuous improvement in all aspects of performance at every level and also upon a greater degree of workforce empowerment.

If goods are made to order within a system of total quality management (TQM), it will have a significant influence on cost bookkeeping and the T accounts exemplified in Section E will be considerably changed.

Closely associated with JIT production system is *backflush costing*. Instead of costs being linked sequentially to products as they move through the production process, they are attached to the output produced on the assumption that such backflushed costs are a realistic measure of the actual costs incurred.

Thus, in backflush accounting, costs are calculated and charged when the completed product is either sold, or transferred (for only a very short period) to finished goods stock.

If products are made as demanded and an efficient JIT purchasing system is in place, there should, in theory, be no stocks of raw materials, work in progress or finished goods. Those that do exist should only be temporary and/or immaterial, for the purpose of preparing financial statements.

An example of basic backflush costing and accounting is now shown:

Material costs for September   £624,000
Conversion costs in that month   £300,000

Advance orders prepared at 1 September   7
Advance orders prepared at 30 September   15
Orders completed and despatched in September   230
Units scrapped in the month   2

With total costs of £924,000, the effective number of units is:

B/F   7
Out   230
Scrap   2
C/F   15

Total 240 and a unit cost of £924,000/240=£3850

Process account			
B/F 7 × 3,850	26,950	Scrap 2 × 3,850	7,700
Costs	924,000	Finished 230 × 3,850	885,500
		C/F 15 × 3,850	57,750
	950,950		950,950

You can see how much simpler the bookkeeping entries are, but this does come at a price of ensuring that the standard costs employed are right up to date and regularly reviewed.

Revision Questions

1   Sweden plc is a manufacturer of "Lindhs". Each Lindh sells for £10 and unit costs are £1.80 for labour; £1.30 for materials and 60p for variable overheads. Fixed Costs per annum are £22,000. The company expects to make and sell 95,000 Lindhs in the next financial year.

Requirements
   (a)   Calulate the breakeven point arithmetically.
   (b)   Reflect all given aspects of production on a conventional breakeven chart.
   (c)   Identify on that chart, the MOS.
   (d)   Draw a profit–volume chart based on all aspects of production.
   (e)   Calculate the C/S ratio, both as a ratio and as a percentage.

2   Denmark plc has three production departments for the manufacture of "splodgetts". Each splodgett passes through each department and in addition, there are two support departments – stores and canteen, which also support each other.

Direct budgeted costs (£'000) for the next financial year are given as:

	A	B	C	Stores	Canteen
Labour	15,900	16,270	8,150	950	1,200
Materials	8,420	11,290	4,400	6,000	7,000
Other	190	0	1,750	225	400

and budgeted overheads for each cost centre are

Indirect wages	4190	3600	2950	170	150

Overheads generally	(£'000)
Machinery insurance	25,000
Power	18,600
Machinery depreciation	5,500
Light and heat	2,700
Rent and rates	2,250
Building insurance	1,970
Rent	3,000
Other	2,280
Total	61,300

Other relevant information that is available is as follows:

	Value of machinery	Area (sq.m)	Power use (%)
Shop A	50,000	4,500	30
Shop B	60,000	5,000	40
Shop C	40,000	5,500	5
Stores	5,000	2,000	15
Canteen	15,000	1,000	10

Production capacity (in hours) in each shop are planned to be:

	Labour	Machine
A	190,000	10,000
B	150,000	20,000
C	60,000	70,000

20% of the stores costs will be apportioned to the canteen and 10% of the canteen costs will be apportioned to the stores. The remainder of each service cost centre expenses, will be apportioned equally between each production shop.

Requirements
(a) Prepare an Overhead Analysis Sheet using your own reasonable choices of apportionment bases (PRATSOOs).
(b) Calculate a relevant OAR for each shop, stating why you have chosen that particular rate.
(c) What quantity of overheads will be absorbed into a job which takes 10 hours in Shop A; 15 hours in Shop B and 5 hours in Shop C?

3   Using the information given for Denmark in Question 2, explain the difference between:

(a) cost centre and cost pools;
(b) apportionment bases and cost drivers.

4   A company named Norway, produces a single product which is based on the following budget, per unit:

Direct labour	£4.50
Direct materials	£2.20
Selling price	£22.70
Variable overhead	£0.80
Fixed overhead	£15, 000 (per month)

The fixed overhead absorption rate is based on producing 8000 units per month. In the current month of April, there was sufficient demand to make and sell only 7500 units.

Requirements
  (a) Produce Operating Statements for April, based on both marginal and absorption costing principles;
  (b) on the basis of the information already given and assuming that 7500 units were produced, but only 7000 were sold, produce two further Operating Statements for April.

5   Explain the principles of backflush costing and accoumting and give FOUR reasons why it has come to prominence in recent years.

6   In deepest Kiev, traditional Ukrainian flower pots are manufactured. The budgeted standard cost for each pot, suitably converted from hryvnyas, is

Labour 30 hours @£6.50	195
Materials 5 kg @£25	125
Variable overheads @£3 per labour hour	90
Fixed overheads per pot	60
Total	£470

Fixed overheads for the year were budgeted to be £300,000 and 5,000 pots were planned to be made and sold at £900 each. Actual fixed overheads turned out to be £320,000, but 5300 pots were made and sold at £895 each. Other actual figures for the year were Labour, 156,000 hours costing £1,050,000; 26,000 kg of material cost £624,000 and variable overheads per labour hour were £2.90.

Requirements
  (a) Calculate all total variances and sub variances for the year.
  (b) Prepare a statement reconciling budgeted profit with actual profit for the year.
  (c) Give possible reasons for each of the variances that you have calculated.

7   Tallinn Ltd manufactures a fluorescent paint. Standard costs, which relate to 200 tins are:

Labour	50 hours @£12	600
Materials	300 kg @£0.70	210
Fixed overheads	50 hours @£2	100

The selling price of a tin is £7 and the monthly production and sales budget is for 12,000 tins. In the month of July 2006, the following actually happened:

Produced and sold	12,400 tins
Sales revenue	£85,560
Materials bought and used	18,400kg cost £12,900
Labour hours	3,087
Labour cost	£38,000
Fixed overheads	£6,400

Requirement

Complete, so far as the information allows, the ledger accounts of Tallinn Ltd and an Operating Statement reconciling budgeted and actual profit for the month.

Tallinn uses standard costs in its integrated accounting system.

.

Solutions to Revision Questions

1   (a) Expected sales are 95,000@£10 = £950,000. Each unit contributes £6.30, so to meet fixed costs of £22,000, we break even when 3492 Lindhs are sold, or when sales revenues reach (3492 × 10) = £34,920.

(b) Follow the conventional breakeven chart on page 15 of this chapter.

2   Denmark: Overhead Analysis Sheet

Expense (£'000)	A	B	C	Stores	Canteen	Total
Indirect wages	4,190	3,600	2,950	170	150	11,060
Machinery insurance	7,355	8,823	5,882	735	2,205	25,000
Power	5,580	7,440	930	2,790	1,860	18,600
Machinery Depreciation	1,617	1,941	1,294	162	486	5,500
L and H	675	750	825	300	150	2,700
R and R	562	625	688	250	125	2,250
Building insurance	492	548	602	218	110	1,970
Rent	750	828	912	340	170	3,000
Other	684	912	114	42	228	2,280
Primary apportionment	21,905	25,467	14,197	5,307	5,484	72,360
Stores apportionment				(1,061)	1,061	–
Canteen apportionment				654	(654)	–
Stores final apportionment	1,633	1,633	1,634	(4,900)	5,891	–
Canteen final apportionment	1,964	1,964	1,963		(5,891)	–
Final apportionment gives	25,502	29,064	17,794	–	–	72,360

(b) Shop A (labour prevelant) £25,502/190, 000hours = £0.134 per labour hour
Shop B (labour prevelant) £29,064/15, 000hours = £0.194 per labour hour
Shop C (machine prevelant) £17,794/70, 000hours = £0.254 per machine hour

(c) $(10 \text{ hours} \times 0.134) + (15 \text{ hours} \times 0.194) + (5 \text{ hours} \times 0.254) = £5.52$

Note: The primary apportionment bases used were machinery book values for machine insurance and depreciation; power utilisation for power and other; Area was used for all the other expenses.

PS So why does the question give us details of direct costs for each of the five cost centres? As a reminder that the total costs of each centre are made up of both direct and indirect, all of which have to be recovered from customers. The direct costs for Shop A have been budgeted on the basis of undertaking 190,000 labour hours and 10,000 hours of machine time. If these hours are met in practice, then all costs will have been recouped.

3   Question 2 was an example of absorption-based costing. The cost centres in Denmark are the three production shops and the two service departments which support the profitable business of producing goods to sell. Since indirect costs cannot be directly coded to individual customer jobs, they are held in these cost centres and are then absorbed into jobs on the basis of an appropriate OAR. That OAR is calculated on an "absorption base", which in the text on page 10, we have called a PRATSOO.

Page 13 of this chapter, under the section titled "Activity Based Recovery Rates", the work of Harvard academics, Kaplan and Norton introduces us to ABC, Activity Based Costing. This uses cost pools instead of cost centres and cost drivers in place of Absorption bases. The financial consequences of using more accurate measures of what caused the overheads in the first place are exemplified in the commentary on ABC.

4   Norway

(a) (i) Operating Statement on Marginal Costing principles

Sales $(7,500 \times 22.70)$	170,250
Variable cost of sales $(7,500 \times 7.50)$	(56,250)
Contribution	114,000
Fixed costs	(15,000)
Operating profit	**99,000**

(ii) on Absorption costing principles

Sales (7,500 × 22.70)		170,250
Cost of sales (7,500 × 9.375)		(70,313)
Operating margin		99,937
Fixed overhead incurred	15,000	
Fixed overheads absorbed		
(7,500 × 1.875)	(14,062)	(938)
Operating profit		**99,000**

Notes: The fixed overheads per unit is calculated as £15,000/8000 = £1.375. The (938) in the second statement above is an under absorption.

(b) Revised Marginal Costing Statement

Sales (7,000 × 22.70)		158,900
Variable Cost of Sales (7,500 × 7.50)	56,250	
Less Stock (500 × 7.50)	3,750	52,500
Contribution		106,400
Fixed costs		(15,000)
Operating profit		**91,400**

Revised Absorption Costing Statement

This is on the same principles as (b) above, but using a unit cost of £9.375. This gives an operating margin of £93,275 and an operating profit of **£92,338**, after deducting the under absorbed overhead. There is an operating profit difference of £938, being 500 units of closing stock at a fixed overheads difference per unit of £1.875. With some unsold stock, a statement on absorption costing principles will always give a higher profit, as some of this year's Fixed Overhead (£1.875 per unit) is carried forward to next year.

5   Backflush accounting is a method of costing a product, where production is based on the JIT philosophy (see page 35). In these circumstances, the valuation of each type of inventory, (raw materials, work in progress and finished goods) becomes less important or immaterial, as raw material is passed straight from supplier to production and finished goods go straight to the customer.

Backflush accounting works backwards. Instead of the laborious use of absorption costing or ABC techniques, costs are allocated between cost of sales and any closing inventory to establish profitability. An example of backflush costing is shown on pages 35–36.

Its prominence is linked to the move away from "make and stock" to more flexible manufacturing systems, based on JIT – make what the customer requires when it is wanted. This initially applies to the procurement of raw materials, as production is regulated by demand "pull", instead of "pushing" ahead with full production regardless. Although this may keep labour and machines fully operative, the consequence may be expensive overstocking of products.

6   Ukrainian Flowerpots

(a) Variance calculations

Labour
Actual hours worked at actual price	1,050,000	
Actual hours at standard price	1,014,000	Rate variance 36,000(A)
Standard hours at standard rate	1,033,500	Efficiency variance 19,500(F)

Materials
As labour but using quantity, not hours

Price variance 26,000(F)
Usage variance 12,500(F)

Variable overhead
As labour

Expenditure variance 15,600(F)
Efficiency variance 9,000(F)

Fixed overhead
Actual cost	320,000	
Budgeted cost	300,000	Expenditure variance 20,000(A)
Standard cost	318,000	Volume variance 18,000(F)
$(5,300 \times 60)$		

(b) Statement Reconciling Budgeted and Actual Profit

Sales margin variance		
Actual sales revenue 5300 × 895	4,743,500	
Standard cost of actual sales volume		
5300 × 470	2,491,000	
	2,252,500	
Budgeted margin		
5000 × (900 − 470)	2,150,000	
	£102,500	
Budgeted profit	2,150,000	
Sales margin variance	102,500	(F)
	2,252,500	
Cost variances (as before)	44,600	(F)
Actual profit	£2,297,100	

CHECK

Actual revenue		4,743,500	
Actual costs			
Lab	1,050,000		
Mat	624,000		
VO	452,400		
FO	320,000	−2,446,400	
Actual profit		£2,297,100	

(c) Labour: extra hourly pay was approved to get a key job done, for which the staff worked their little socks off and saved valuable time.

Materials:we used less than expected and but were still able to get a special discount on the quantity bought.

The standard cost of variable overheads per hour, was slightly less than planned (a bad estimate!) and fewer hours were worked.

An increase in the budgeted cost of the factory business rates was due to the result of a revaluation and the fixed overhead expenditure was greater as a result. The good news was that an extra, unbudgeted, 300 pots were sold and each one brought in an additional £60.

7   Tallinn Ltd

This question is designed to show competence in cost book keeping. In this case, as the text indicated (page 40), the cost ledger is kept on standard costs. It does not require the calculation of variances, which may therefore appear as a single "balancing" total in the Operating Statement (which is called for).

The variances have however been calculated by the author and if you wish to check the total figure of 880(A), you may follow the pattern in Question 6. You can confirm your answers with those set out in the Operating Statement, which also follows that pattern exactly and in summary, looks like this:

Budgeted profit	29,400
Total sales margin variance	(260)
Cost variances	(880)
Actual profit	**£28,260**

The relevant T accounts in Tallinn's cost ledger would appear as below:

Wages control account			
Cash paid	38,000	Work in progress	37,044
		Labour rate	
		variance	956

Raw material control account			
Creditors	12,900	Work in progress	12,880
		Material price	
		variance	20

Production overheads control account			
Creditor	6,400	Expenditure variance	400
Volume variance	200	Work in progress	6,200

Work in progress control account			
Labour	37,044	Cost of sales	56,420
Materials	12,880		
Labour efficiency	156		
Materials usage	140		
Production	6,200		
Overheads			

Profit and loss account

Cost of sales	56,420	Sales	85,560
Adverse variances		Favourable variances	
Labour price	956	Labour efficiency	156
Material price	20	Material usage	140
Overheads expenditure	400	Overhead volume	200
Profit	28,260		
	86,056		**86,056**

Financial Accounting
and Reporting

To give an accurate and exhaustive account of that period, would need a far less brilliant pen than mine

(Max Beerbohm)

A   Syllabus Overview

CIMA is the premier qualification for management accountants. Not surprisingly, the syllabus is based on management accounting. Six of the ten papers forming the CIMA professional qualification, have the term "management accounting" in their title and all but two, include the word "management".

The two "missing" Papers are P7 and P8 and they provide the financial accounting knowledge that a Chartered Management Accountant should possess.

Paper P7 contains a 20% share of the syllabus to deal with the principles of business taxation. Because of its specialised nature, this subject is NOT included in this Guide. The remainder of P7 is concerned with financial reporting (10%); the financial aspects of a single company (45%) and the management of short-term finance (25%).

Paper P8 extends this knowledge to the financial statements of a group of companies (35%) with a similar percentage for analysing and interpreting financial statements. The balance is related to the measurement of income and capital and developments in financial reporting.

Before looking in more detail at the P7 syllabus, it is assumed that the student has a good basic knowledge of bookkeeping and accounting, the structure of the main financial statements of a company and the principles of the regulatory regime, which underpins financial reporting.

The syllabus for the CBA Paper CO2, "Framework of Financial Accounting", apart from dealing with the basics of accounting records and systems, prepares accounts and financial reports for single entities. The principles, covered in all of these areas, are then further developed in P7. The two other CO2 syllabus topics are the Regulatory Framework (considered in this chapter) and auditing principles, which are touched on in Chapter 3.

One aspect of basic financial accounting which the student may well need to use at Managerial Level, is the use of T accounts, to calculate actual cash flows in an accounting period. Provided that you can keep and close a set of books and prepare the main financial statements for a company from a trial balance with the usual list of year end adjustments, getting started in P7 should not be a problem. The main issues then will be getting used to the recently changed structure of the principal statements and, especially, knowledge of the impact of the relevant International Accounting Standards (IAS), which underpin those statements. This chapter will centre around a practical knowledge of the relevant IAS.

The syllabus summary for P7, is as follows:

A Principles of Business Taxation
B Regulation of Financial Reporting
C Single Company Financial Accounts
D Managing Short-Term Finance

In syllabus Section C, there is a requirement to know the rules (accounting standards) inherent in preparing published accounts. Those standards which are specifically in the current P7 syllabus are

IAS 1, 2, 7, 8, 10, 11, 14, 16, 17, 18, 23, 24, 32, 35, 36, 37, 38 and 39

Below is a cross-referenced list of all current International and UK Accounting Standards.

1 Extant UK and International Accounting Standards

United Kingdom

SSAP 4, 5, 9, 13, 19, 20, 21 and 25

FRS 1, 2, 3, 5, 6, 7, 8, 9, 10, 11, 12, 15, 16, 17, 18, 19, 20, 21, 22, 23, 24, 25 26, 27, 28 and 29

International

IAS 1, 2, 5, 7, 8, 10, 11, 12, 14, 16, 17, 18, 19, 20, 21, 23, 24, 26, 27, 28, 29, 30, 31, 32, 33, 34, 36, 37, 38, 39, 40 and 41

IFRS 1, 2, 3, 4, 5, 6, 7 and 8

Where are they now?

SSAP	IAS	IFRS
4	20*	
5		
9	2, 11*	
13	38***	

19	40*	
20		2***
21	17**	
25	(14)	8***
FRS		
1	7***	
2	27**	
3	(8)	5*
4	39***	
5	27**	
6		3***
7		3***
8	24**	
9	28**	
10		3***
11	36**	
12	37*	
13		7**
15	16***	
16	12**	
17	19***	
18	1, 8**	
19	12***	
20		2*
21	10*	
22	33*	
23	21*	
24	29*	
25	33*	
26	39**	
27		4***
28	1**	
29		7*

The asterisks are intended to give an indication of the extent of change made to the original UK Standard. (* minor, to *** significant).

Finally, this chapter will look at other documents and bodies which are relevant to the Standard setting process and recent developments in financial reporting, including the Companies Act 2006, the first major piece of comprehensive legislation affecting companies in 20 years.

B   The Regulatory Framework

The present machinery and standards

The Regulatory Framework in the United Kingdom, prior to 2001, was under the overall responsibility of the Financial Reporting Council (FRC). Within the FRC's umbrella, Statements of Standard Accounting Practice (SSAP) and Financial Reporting Standards (FRS) were issued by the Accounting Standards Board (ASB). 25 SSAPs and 29 FRSs were eventually issued. The FRC machinery also included the Financial Reporting Review Panel (FRRP) to ensure compliance with Standards and the Urgent Issues Task Force (UITF), to deal with and give authoritative advice on emerging issues.

That set-up continues today, although the ASB does not issue any further Standards, unless they are the same as those published by the International Accounting Standards Board (IASB). The IASB replaced, in April 2001, the IAS Committee, which was established in 1973, to publish IASs, with the aim of bringing together Standards on a worldwide basis. The European Commission subsequently issued a Directive that, within the EU, all consolidated accounts of listed companies must be prepared under International Standards for all accounting periods ending on or after 1 January 2005. The IASC, having issued 41 Standards, gave way to the IASB whose outputs are entitled IFRSs. All initials, is it not?!

The UK's ASB has agreed to bring its Standards into line with international requirements, but this will take time, as will obtaining worldwide approval to a common set of documents. Is such an objective reasonably attainable, given the range of different economies, religions, etc.?

We now therefore have a mixture of standards operating in the United Kingdom; 8SSAPs, 26FRSs, 32IASs and 8IFRSs.

The IASB is responsible for working up a new standard, from an initial Exposure Draft. It is assisted in its standard setting role, by the Standards Advisory Council (whose main take is to advise the Board on work priorities) and the International Financial Reporting Interpretations Committee (IFRIC), which issues interpretive guidance on the practical application of the IFRSs.

There have been some recent developments in financial reporting these include Sarbanes–Oxley Act and Operating and Financial Review (OFR).

Sarbanes–Oxley Act 2002

The final paragraphs of Chapter 3, deal with this piece of US legislation, enacted after recent American financial scandals. It introduced onerous new disclosure rules, which affected UK companies having contact with the United States. Important recent developments surrounding this detailed law, have all been designed to ease compliance with Sarbox. In May 2007, the SEC Commissioners approved measures which suggested that a more "principles-based" approach to financial regulation is gaining ground in the United States. At the same time, a new auditing standard, AS5, was issued, to reduce overzealous audit checks of internal controls.

The Operating and Financial Review

Issued by the ASB in 1993, the permissive OFR was designed to encourage the development of best practice in providing an open discussion and commentary on the main factors/uncertainties facing a particular company. This was to be done in a style which did not require the publication of material that could be advantageous to competitors. A report by The Company Law Review Steering Committee in July 2001 proposed that there should be a new, mandatory OFR and that it should contain both a director's review of operations and finances and a discussion of current main trends and a view of the future.

The result of deliberations on this document was the issue of a revised OFR in January 2003. The Government then required all listed companies to publish an OFR as from 1 April 2005, to be compliant with a standard to be issued by the ASB. This Standard appeared as OFR Reporting Standard RS1 in May 2005, and it contained the following seven guiding principle that the OFR should:

1 reflect the directors' view of the business;
2 focus on matters that are relevant to investors in assessing the strategies adopted and the potential for those strategies to succeed. Whilst maintaining the primacy of meeting investors' needs, directors should take a "broad view" in deciding what should be included in their OFR, on the grounds that the decisions and agendas of other stakeholders can influence the performance and value of a company;
3 have a forward-looking orientation with an analysis of the main trends and factors which are likely to affect the entity's future development, performance and position;

4 complement as well as supplement the financial statements with additional explanations of amounts included in the financial statements;

5 be comprehensive and understandable but avoid the inclusion of too much information that is not directly relevant;

6 be balanced and neutral – in this way the OFR can produce reliable information;

7 be comparable over time – the ability to compare with other entities in the same industry or sector is encouraged.

RS 1 then set out the following key elements of what the OFR should cover:

- the nature, objectives and strategies of the business;
- the development and performance of the business, both in the period and in the future;
- the resources, risks and uncertainties and relationships that may affect value; and
- the position of the business including a description of the capital structure objectives and liquidity of the entity, both in the period under review and the future

It is for directors to consider how best to use this framework to structure the operating and financial circumstances of the entity.

Source: www.frc.org.uk

and the qualities that it should have:

- a forward-looking orientation;
- complement as well as supplement the financial statements;
- be comprehensive and understandable;
- be balanced and neutral; and
- be comparable over time.

Source: www.frc.org.uk

Many public companies issue an OFR either as a separate document, or as part of the Annual Report.

The framework for the preparation and presentation of financial statements (1989)

Although the ASB was established and issued its first UK SSAP in 1970, it was not until 1989 that it published guidance to ensure consistency in its published Standards. The Framework set out a number of key principles which should underpin financial reporting and, of course, shortly after its appearance, the ASB's output was effectively overtaken by the development of International Standards!

The Framework contains four main sets of guidance:

1 The objective of financial statements
2 Qualitative characteristics of financial information
3 The elements of financial statements
4 Concepts of capital and capital maintenance

Looking briefly at each of them:

1 An Annual Report should meet the needs of stakeholders, in both assessing the adequacy of the Directors' stewardship and in making economic decisions. Seven users of accounts and their specific requirements are identified;
2 The information in an Annual Report should be relevant (up to the date and current), reliable (free from material error or bias), comparable (standard information may be easily compared) and understandable to the person on the Clapham omnibus;
3 There are definitions of five main elements; three relating to the Balance Sheet (asset, liability and equity) and two – incomes and expenses – relating to the Income Statement. Guidance is given on various measurement bases (e.g. historic cost, current cost) that determine the monetary amounts at which the elements may appear;
4 Concepts of capital and capital maintenance, deal with the impact of inflation on the measurement of profit and values.

Despite the earlier comment about the unfortunate timing of the issue of the framework, the ASB's document has been of great assistance to the IASB in the development of harmonised International Standards. Also, to readers of accounts and to auditors, who can now examine published statements knowing that they have been produced against an agreed and rigorous set of key principles.

At this point, it is worth mentioning two documents. Firstly, the publication, in July 2003, of IFRS1 entitled "First Time Adoption of International Financial Reporting Standards". This gives detailed guidance on the preparation of the first annual statement which an entity publishes under international standards and on compliance with such Standards subsequently. Of much more practical importance, is the revision, in December 2003, of IAS1 "Presentation of Financial Information" (originally "Presentation of Financial Statements").

This document should be compulsory reading for all P7 candidates, dealing as it does, with the contents of the four main financial statements and the explanatory Notes thereto, including a summary of significant accounting policies. A copy is included as Appendix C, beginning on page 195.

Other bodies and documents

Finally before leaving this section on the regulation of financial reporting, it is worth mentioning some terms relating to other bodies and documents, which you will meet in the course of your studies:

SORP (Statement of Recommended Practice) is a set of accounting standards for a specific sector of the economy (e.g. local government, universities), which follow relevant published standards and have been approved by the ASB.

CCAB (Consultative Committee of Accountancy Bodies) is a gathering of representatives from each of the six main UK accountancy bodies, to discuss matters common to the profession and to speak with a unified voice.

GAAP (Generally Accepted Accounting Practice) is defined in the CIMA *Official Terminology* as comprising components of company law; the ASB's accounting Standards UITF Abstracts; SORPS; the Stock Exchange Listing Rules (yellow book) of the Financial Services Authority and periodic recommendations and pronouncements of the FRRP.

IOSCO (International Organization of Securities Commissions) is a body ensuring consistency of stock market regulations between countries, with a view to protecting investors. A set of core standards was issued in December 1998. the UK Stock Exchange and the US Securities and Exchange Commission (SEC) are key members of this body.

FRSSE   (Financial Reporting Standard for Smaller Entities) is a separate comprehensive set of standards applicable to smaller companies as currently defined, by reference to turnover, assets or number of employees. There is also a separate ASB document incorporating both legal and accounting requirements for small companies in one place. The IASB is at present developing an IFRS for both small- and medium-sized companies. (An Exposure Draft of proposals is out for comment until 1 October 2005).

FASB   (Financial Accounting Standards Board), is the US equivalent of the ASB.

OFR   (The Operating and Financial Review). A document to complement the Annual Report of a company. A brief history and details were presented earlier in this chapter.

NORWALK   (Integration of International and US Accounting Standards). At their joint meeting in Norwalk, Connecticut, USA on 18, September 2002, the Financial Accounting Standards Board (FASB) and the International Accounting Standards Board (IASB) each acknowledged their commitment to the development of high-quality, compatible accounting standards that could be used for both domestic and cross-border financial reporting. At that meeting, both the FASB and IASB pledged to use their best efforts to (a) make their existing financial reporting standards fully compatible as soon as is practicable and (b) to co-ordinate their future work programmes to ensure that once achieved, compatibility is maintained. Differences between IAS and US accounting Standards are still "some way off" according to research results published by Ernst and Young early in 2007. Cessation of the current requirement to reconcile two sets of accounts might be possible by 2009 according to the Securities and Exchange Commission, in a linked statement.

C Single Company Financial Accounts

This is the main section of Chapter 2 and is concerned with the application of specific syllabus standards, to the preparation of the main financial statements. During their P7 studies, students will, no doubt, have plenty of practice in preparing these statements from a trial balance and supporting notes. Relevant standards mentioned in the syllabus, are now summarised in a standard format:

IAS 1 – Presentation of Financial Statements

Main purpose	To prescribe the basis for the presentation of general purpose financial statements
	Revised in December 2003 as Appendix C
Impact	Sets out the format and main contents of the principal Financial Statements and Notes thereto
Equivalent	FRS18 – Accounting Policies; FRS 3 FRS 28
Study guidance	• Get to know the layout of the main statements and the wording of the Notes relating to the accounting policies
	• Obtain and study the Annual Reports of a number of companies

IAS 2 – Inventories (Revised December 2003)

Main purpose	To set out the accounting treatment for inventories and their measurement at the lower of cost and net realisable value
Impact	Determines the value of Inventories for the purpose of calculating cost of sales in an Income Statement and Inventories as a Balance Sheet Current Asset
Equivalent	SSAP9 – Stocks and Long-Term Contracts
Study guidance	• Know the definitions of cost and net realisable value
	• Be able to calculate the total value of an inventory using accepted methods

IAS 7 – Cash Flow Statements

Main purpose	To show the generation and use of cash resources in an entity under the three separate headings of operating activities, investing and financing
Impact	Requires the preparation of one of the principal financial statements. Analyses the movement of cash and cash equivalents between balance sheets and gives a clearer appreciation of the relationship between total cash flows and those of prescribed component parts
Equivalent	FRS1 – Title as above
Study guidance	• Know both the basic and expanded headings
	• Be able to prepare a statement on both direct and indirect methods

IAS 8 – Accounting Policies, Changes in Accounting Estimates and Errors (December 2003)

Main purpose	To prescribe the criteria for selecting and changing accounting policies together with the disclosure and accounting treatment of changes in policies, estimates and correction of errors
Impact	The determination and disclosure of accounting policies is required to be set out in Notes to the Financial Statements. Such policies inform the reader what options the entity has chosen, where there are choices. The standard also requires the restating of comparatives for prior periods under specific circumstances
Equivalent	FRS3 – Reporting Financial Performance; FRS18
Study guidance	• Study Annual Reports Accounting Policies Notes • Be aware of the circumstances in which a change of policy requires a prior year adjustment • Know when correction of errors requires prior year adjustments • What is an error and what is an estimate?

IAS 10 – Events after the Balance Sheet Date (December 2003)

Main purpose	To remove dividends declared after the Balance Sheet date as adjusting events
Impact	The previous division between adjusting and non-adjusting events is still applicable. Similarly dividends received from associates/subsidiaries relating to a period prior to the Balance Sheet date are also, now, non-adjusting
Equivalent	FRS21 – Title as above
Study guidance	• Know the regular lists of adjusting and non-adjusting events • Remember the importance of materiality in making adjustments • If in doubt, add a suitable note (will a reader be well informed otherwise?)

IAS 11 – Construction and Service Contracts (Revised 1993)

Main purpose	Revenues and costs associated with a construction contract should be included in the financial statements by reference to the stage of completion of the contract
Impact	This continues the long established principle, set out in the second part of SSAP9, for a gradual "taking" of the profit on a long-term contract. Any foreseeable loss should be recognised immediately (a good example of prudence in action)
Equivalent	SSAP9 – Stocks and Long-Term Contracts
Study guidance	• There are different approaches to calculating annual figures. Get used to a particular method and always bear prudence in mind – don't build up too much profit, before the contract outcome is certain

IAS 14 – Segment Reporting (1997) (now IFRS 8 Operating Segments)

Main purpose	To give users of accounts a better appreciation of the geographical and product make-up of certain consolidated figures
Impact	An example of the layout of a segmented analysis is set out below. You will see that it contains a great deal more information about specific "segments" of a business than total financial statement figures. Such analysis is invaluable in helping to understand an entity's risks and returns
Equivalent	SSAP25 – Segmental Reporting (now IFRS 8)
Study guidance	• Study and be able to draft, a segment format. • Understand that the main purpose of segmenting is to better appreciate stewardship and degrees of risk (eggs in one basket!) • The issue of IFRS 8 in November 2006, contains a notable change in shifting presentation from the traditional emphasis on product and geographical sectors to managerial segments based on the internal structure of the company. The European Commission is seeking further comment from a wide range of interested parties before making an endorsement report to the European Parliament in September 2007.

IAS 16 – Property, Plant and Equipment (Revised December 2003)

Main purpose	To prescribe the accounting treatment for property, plant and equipment. In particular, the standard deals with the initial definition of cost, carrying amounts and subsequent depreciation/impairment charges.
Impact	A key standard, as it deals with major aspects of non current assets, an area so wide that an examination question requiring knowledge of the standard is guaranteed.
Equivalent	FRS 15 (Tangible Fixed Assets) and FRS 11 (Impairment of Fixed Assets and Goodwill)
Study guidance	Know what is include/excluded in the standard, the treatment of borrowing costs and the measurement rules after initial Balance Sheet recognition.

IAS 17 – Leases (Revised December 2003)

Main purpose	To prescribe for both lessors and lessees the accounting policies and disclosures to apply to both operating and finance leases
Impact	A source of good questions for P7 candidates, particularly the methods of apportioning the lease payments. The standard also has implications for the Balance Sheet value of assets held under a finance lease
Equivalent	SSAP21 – Accounting for Leases and Hire Purchase Contracts
Study guidance	<ul><li>Be confident about making the correct entries in each set of books</li><li>Know the disclosure requirements for lessees, which are a bit complicated</li><li>Know the apportionment methods and use the simplest if you have a choice</li></ul>

IAS 18 – Revenue (1993)

Main purpose	Deals with the requirements to be satisfied before revenue should be recognised in Income Statements
Impact	The original guidance was as a Note Supplementary to FRS5 – Reporting the Substance of Transactions. The new standard seeks to give much clearer guidance on when revenue from sales or service transactions, should be recognised in financial statements (i.e. when performance is satisfied)

Equivalent	FRS5 – Revenue Recognition; SSAP 9 (Appendix G)
Study guidance	• Understand the reasons why revenue recognition is such an important current issue
	• Know the circumstances under which different types of revenue might prudently be included in the Income Statement

IAS 23 – Borrowing Costs (Revised December 2003)

Main purpose	To prescribe the accounting treatment for borrowing costs
Impact	Borrowing costs should be charged directly as an expense but may be capitalised if directly attributable to the acquisition, construction or production of a qualifying asset
Equivalent	FRS 15 Tangible Fixed Assets (part)
Study guidance	• Be aware of the strict circumstances in which borrowing costs may be included as part of the capital cost
	• Know how to calculate the capitalisation rate

IAS 24 – Related Party Disclosures (December 2003)

Main purpose	To highlight the possibility that related parties may have influenced the business transactions of an entity
Impact	Requires the identifying relationships and parties concerned to be disclosed. Financial statements are prepared on the assumption of an "arms length" basis to all transactions. This standard spells out disclosure where this is not the case
Equivalent	FRS8 – Related Policy Disclosures
Study guidance	• Know the provided lists of those who are, or who are assumed by implication to be, related parties
	• Know the disclosure provisions by types of transaction and for key management personnel, compensation
	• In February 2007, the IASB published new proposals for entities to disclose, in financial statements, information about related parties. The main change proposed is to reduce the disclosure requirements in IAS 24, that some entities are related only because they are each State controlled, or are significantly influenced by the State

IAS 32 – Financial Instruments: Disclosure and Presentation

Main Purpose	To present information in a way that distinguishes financial instruments between equity and liabilities and transactions consequent upon such liabilities (e.g. dividends)
Impact	The recent substantial growth in the use of new instruments, especially forms of derivatives, has required guidance so that shareholders can have a greater appreciation of the use of such instruments and of the associated risks
Equivalent	FRS25 – Title as above; FRS 29
Study Guidance	• Know the types of financial instrument to which this Standard applies and the types of risk to which they may be exposed • The disclosure requirements are very considerable and will need a personal method of learning them • This Standard and IAS 39, also cover important aspects of the issue, redemption and repurchase of shares by an entity

IAS 35 – Discontinuing Operations (now IFRS 5 Discontinued Operations)

Main Purpose	To present separately the assets and liabilities of an operation which is held for sale.
Impact	When a discontinued operation has been disposed of, there will be no Balance Sheet items to present or represent. The Income Statement requires only one figure for discontinued operations, with supplementary disclosures in the Notes.
Equivalent	FRS 3 Reporting Financial Performance
Study Guidance	• Get to know the criteria to be classified as a "held for sale component", as representing a major line of business or geographical area of operations.

IAS 36 – Impairment of Assets

Main Purpose	Prescribes the requirements to be observed to ensure that assets are carried at no more than their recoverable amount
Impact	If an asset is carried above its future use or sale value, an impairment loss should be recognised immediately. The Standard sets out sequential stages to be followed in calculating whether or not an asset may be impaired

Equivalent	FRS11 – Impairment of Fixed Assets and Goodwill
Study Guidance	• Be able to list and understand the four sequential stages
	• Know how to calculate the extent of the impairment and how to reflect component losses in the published accounts

IAS 37 – Provisions, Contingent Liabilities and Contingent Assets

Main Purpose	Sets out the accounting and disclosure requirements for the majority of provisions, contingent liabilities and contingent assets
Impact	Requires determination of the extent to which a future liability is probable (create a provision) or possible (a contingent liability Note) contingent assets may only be recognised under strict arrangements
Equivalent	FRS12 – As above
Study Guidance	• Be able to define and recognise types of obligation and the difference between a provision and a contingency
	• Make best estimates measuring the amount of a disclosure
	• Know the disclosures required in each case

IAS 38 – Intangible Assets

Main Purpose	Prescribes the accounting treatment of certain intangible assets, particularly goodwill, research and development
Impact	The strict requirements for carrying an intangible asset are set out, as are the rules for its valuation and the disclosures required. To be capitalised, an intangible asset must be identifiable, control a resource and generate future economic benefits
Equivalent	SSAP13 – Accounting for Research and Development; FRS10
Study Guidance	• Recall the well-established SECTOR mnemonic for circumstances under which development costs may be capitalised
	• Know the list of assets to which the Standard does not apply
	• Know the ways of determining the useful life for different intangible assets

IAS 39 – Financial Instruments: Recognition and Measurement	
Main Purpose	Sets out the principles for recognising and measuring financial assets and liabilities
Impact	The standard applies to all financial instruments, except for certain specified. It defines different types of instrument and the ways in which each may be valued for reporting purposes
Equivalent	FRS26 – Financial Instruments: Measurement: FRS 4 and 5
Study Guidance	• Know the types of instrument to which the standard applies and does not apply • Know the requirements for initial and subsequent measurement • Be aware of the processes for applying the standard rather than the practical implementation (which requires specialised knowledge)

D Managing Short-Term Finance

The final section of the P7 syllabus, covers the Learning Aim that students should be able to "assess the short-term financial requirements for a business entity". This section is therefore all about the management of liquidity, and working capital. The CIMA *Official Terminology* defines liquidity as the availability of sufficient funds to meet financial commitments as they fall due. Working capital is that which is available for the day to day operations of a business and is normally, the excess of current assets over current liabilities. (CIMA *Official Terminology*).

The CIMA CBA syllabus for Paper CO2, does not contain a specific reference to these issues, concerning itself with those aspects of short-term financial management, which relate to the calculation and basic interpretation of well-known ratios – current, acid test, stock turnover, debtor and creditor management. There are test questions at the end of this chapter on all of these, just to ensure that you are up to speed with them!

P7 takes the study of working capital somewhat further. A key ingredient of the details of the syllabus, is the preparation and practical management of a cash forecast and that is covered, as a feature of the Master Budget, in Chapter 5 of this book. Since your study text for P7 will deal with all these "new" matters in some detail, it is only necessary here to take a more co-ordinated look at those aspects of working capital (the ratios mentioned above) that you should already have met.

The two main short-term liquidity ratios are the current ratio:

Current assets/current liabilities = £150,000/£80,000 = 1.875:1

And the acid test (liquidity, quick) ratio (which excludes the inventory of £80,000):

Current assets/current liabilities = £70,000/£80,000 = 1.875:1

Both ratios are expressed as $x:1$. Many textbooks will suggest that the ideal ratios should be 2:1 and 1:1, respectively, but these are very broad measures which do not take the type of business, or particular circumstances into account. Our calculations above would not look too good in a set of published league tables! In this simple example, the relationship may have been perfectly acceptable over many years, and not as a result of overstocking.

The inventory turnover, in times per year, divides the cost of sales by average inventory (opening plus closing divided by 2). Debtor days divides average trade debtors by total credit sales and multiplied by 365 and the time taken to pay trade creditors divides average trade creditors by credit purchases and multiplied by 365 to convert it into days. All good simple stuff!

Let us assume that the results of our calculations give an annual inventory turn of 3.75 times. That equates to $365/3.75 = 97.3$ days. Our debtor days figure is 94 and we pay our trade creditors every 175 days. Herein of course, lies the basis of a good cash flow – get the cash in well before you pay it out! On the face of it, however, none of these figures reflect good cash or business management.

At the Managerial Level, you will be required to consider these elements together, as the Working Capital cycle, defined as the time between receiving goods for sale and when the cash for those sales actually arrives. This gives us:

Inventory turnover	97
Debtor days	94
	191
Creditor days	(175)
Length of cycle	16 days (nice work if you can get it!)

Definitions of each of these three terms need refinement and handling with care, depending on the type of business being considered. The timing of stock turnover will be very different between a supermarket and a company making and selling grand pianos. Comparison of standard internal figures, or with a similar competitor, over a period of years, will be a more useful guide to performance in the management of working capital.

To reinforce these comments and calculations, consider the two following situations, A and B and comment on the performance in each:

A Internal comparison

	This year ratio	Last year ratio
Current	6.2:1	9.5:1
Acid test	3.7:1	3.7:1
Inventory turnover	86 days	3 times
Debtor days	49 days	50
Creditor days	37 days	65

B External comparison for latest year

	You	Rival A	Rival B	National average
Debtor days	59	36	68	57
Creditor days	64	36	76	70

C Different industries comparision

		Non-current assets (%)	Inventory (%)	Cash (%)
A	Supermarket chain	5	5	65
B	Food processor	60	5	15
C	Building society	30	30	5

Here we have three different types of business, with Balance Sheet extracts shown as percentages of Total Assets. Unfortunately, each set of figures has been placed against the wrong letter. Suggest which set of figures belongs against each letter and be prepared to explain your selection.

In the opening paragraphs of this section, there was a reference to the preparation and management of cash budgets in Chapter 5. In that chapter, we will see how a forecast of cash flows, to supplement the annual budget is critical in assessing when there will be surplus cash (for profitable investment) and when there will be a need for the borrowing of money or resort to a bank overdraft, to plug a liquidity shortfall.

The regular preparation and scrutiny of these basic ratios and calculation of the working capital cycle will be valuable steps in maximising investment return and minimising the payment of overdraft or loan interest. These issues will be considered further in the later chapter.

Readings

Developments in Financial Reporting

2009 and the next batch of IFRS

An excellent article by Nick Topazio, a CIMA technical specialist, appeared in the February 2007 edition of the CIMA journal *Financial Management*. This is set out below.

The next batch of IFRS won't kick in till 2009, but there's no reason to sit back and wait for them. **Nick Topazio** explains how CIMA members can shape the standards.

Having largely overcome the problems of adopting international financial reporting standards (IFRS) from 2005, listed companies in the EU called on the international Accounting Standards Board (IASB) for a period of stability to help the bedding-in process. In response, it has announced that no new standard it issues will take effect before January 1, 2009. Those involved in preparing financial reports might be forgiven for thinking that they're over the worst, out it wouldn't be surprising if the issues of implementing new IFRS in 2009 turn out to be as tough as they were in 2005.

The IASB will continue to amend existing standards and it's working on several projects that are due to come to fruition before 2009. These include five exposure drafts, four discussion papers and the following eight new standards:

- Borrowing costs.
- Segmental reporting.
- Business combinations.
- Financial statement presentation.
- Joint ventures.
- Taxation.
- IFRS for SMEs.
- Liabilities.

These will affect nearly all areas of reporting and implementation problems will inevitably arise.

Each IASB project (apart from the first four standards listed above) presents opportunities for interested parties to influence the outcome – and now is the time to start doing so. CIMA's responses to IASB consultations are more persuasive when they contain the insights of its members, who shouldn't comprise only current IFRS reporters. IFRS has already become relevant to AIM-listed firms, while the Accounting Standards Board is converging UK standards with IFRS. Indeed, the UK is likely to adopt the forthcoming IFRS for SMEs to some degree, which will increase the number of entities that apply IFRS.

Even those financial managers who aren't directly involved in reporting are unlikely to escape being affected by new IFRS principles. The new segmental reporting standard demonstrates the overlap between management accounting and financial accounting: IFRS8 requires that a firm's external reports analyse financial performance into those segments that are used to manage the business. To the extent that non-Gaap figures – e.g., Ebitda and operating profit – are also used in management decision-making in relation to these segments, these need to be disclosed and reconciled back to the IFRS statements. As a result, I expect that professionals who are responsible for internal segmental reporting will need to be aware of the external standard's requirements.

IFRS are sometimes seen as too theoretical and difficult to implement. Professional accountants in business are in an ideal position to reflect on proposals for changes and offer practical suggestions for easing their implementation. CIMA members can play an important role in improving future standards by sharing their experience with the standard-setters.

Nick Topazio is a CIMA technical specialist.

How to Get Involved in CIMA's Community of Practice

CIMA is committed to gathering members' views on financial reporting developments before it responds to consultations. It does this via the financial reporting development group (practitioners who meet about three times a year) and its consultations database (www.cimaglobal.com/cdb). This contains details of past and present consultations, including summaries of proposals, a members' comment facility and, in the case of completed consultations, links to the institute's responses.

To facilitate even wider member participation in this process, CIMA is expanding its community of practice to include an online discussion forum on financial reporting. The forum is designed to encourage members to share their ideas, resources and learning.

The community of practice focuses on how accountants in business can contribute to the development of financial reporting standards, regulations and best practice. Participants in an active community can benefit from:

- Timely, relevant and cost-effective CPD.
- Access to wider expertise and alternative views.
- The sharing and development of good practice.
- The ability to experiment with new ideas, tools and techniques in a safe environment.
- Networking and benchmarking opportunities.

The financial reporting community of practice will initially run for a six-month pilot period. We will then review activity and seek feedback from participants. CIMA has invited members to join whom it believes, based on the details they have provided about their jobs and employers, will be able to provide useful insights. If you are a member who believes that you could contribute to the community, please e-mail tis@cimaglobal.com for further information.

Real Time Financial Reporting

The *Financial Times* for 8 November 2006, contained a report by its Financial Correspondent, Barney Jopson, on proposals supported by six major accounting firms. That article is reproduced below. This also shows the envisaged New Model of Corporate Reporting.

Accountancy firms map out new world

The new IFRS regulations have caused concern in the sector but the industry leaders have their own ideas, writes **Barney Jopson**

When Lord Browne, BP chief executive, presented the oil group's annual results to investors in February, he expressed a rising tide of anger over the effect of new accounting standards.

"Some would argue that International Financial Reporting Standards neither produce a record of the accountability of management, nor a measure of the changes in the economic value of assets and liabilities," he said. "I would agree with them. What IFRS actually does is make our results more difficult to understand."

His words crystallised the discontent of companies. For the first time last week, a powerful coalition of investors – the International Corporate Governance

Network – articulated its worries about accounting. And another watershed moment will occur today.

The world's six biggest accounting firms are due to publish proposals – the most comprehensive so far – for a new model of corporate reporting in a bid to press regulators and policymakers into action.

Their ideas, if adopted, would effectively consign 20th century accounting to the dustbin, and free Lord Browne and others from the anachronistic task of presenting static results in line with the cycles of the Gregorian calendar.

"We all believe the current model is broken," said Mike Rake, chairman of KPMG International. "We're not in a very happy situation."

PwC, Deloitte, KPMG, Ernst & Young, Grant Thornton and BDO plan to unveil a series of ideas in an unprecedented joint paper today and two points standout. First, they say quarterly and annual reporting should be superseded by real-time, internet-based reporting, enabling investors to get whatever information they want whenever they want it.

'We all believe
the current
model is broken.
We're not in a
very happy
situation'
**MIKE RAKE,
KPMG**

"Such a system should give users the same choices and abilities to access relevant business information as consumers and producers now have when purchasing goods and services over the internet," the paper says.

Investors, the accountants note, would have to accept that more frequent disclosures would come with different levels of assurance from traditional financial statements.

The second proposal is to shift corporate reporting away from purely financial data toward wider information that could provide insight into a company's performance and prospects.

Consider a retailer that reports strong income growth on the back of overseas expansion, say the accountants, but which is nonetheless experiencing a decline in repeat purchases by customers. "The latter statistic could well be the proverbial canary in the mine shaft that would signal to investors the company's stock merits a 'sell' rather than a 'buy'," the paper says. Uncharacteristically for accountants, the paper is long on idealism and short on detail. But the spirit of the proposals is likely to be cheered by investors and analysts.

Many stock marketwatchers already devote hours to deconstructing results and feeding the elements into their own preferred valuation models. An officially endorsed system to help them would be welcome.

Some would argue it already exists in the form of an Extensible Business Reporting Language, which allows corporate data to be "tagged" into different categories. But it has been slow to take off. The greatest resistance to the proposals is likely to come from corporate clients. To companies, quarterly reporting has the advantage of allowing them to craft a careful narrative to accompany their figures.

In a data free-for-all, they would either lose control of the narrative entirely, or be forced to spend an inordinate amount of time responding to analysts, bloggers and journalists.

For accountants themselves, this would signal a radical change to their bread-and-butter business. But the six have confidently identified money-spinning opportunities in the "brave new world" they map out.

Accountants would be needed to audit the technology that produces corporate information and the reliability of "tagging" systems, they say. To tackle fraud more effectively, they suggest all public companies be subject to a costly "forensic audit" akin to a police probe every few years.

New Model of Corporate Reporting	
CURRENT SYSTEM	**PROPOSED SYSTEM**
• Quarterley reporting	• Real-time reporting
• Accounts in standardised format	• User-customised statements
• Income statements	• Measures of innovation and customer satisfaction
• Balance sheets	• Looser assessments of intangible and other assets

Revision Questions

1   IAS 1 prescribes the basis of presentation for four general purpose financial statements. An appendix to the standard sets out the minimum headings for these statements.

Requirements
   (a) Draft these statements.
   (b) What are the minimum disclosures required by IAS 1, in respect of explanatory Notes?

2   The trial balance of Tannhauser plc shows the following balances as at 30 June 2005 (£'000):

Sales revenue		1,600
Share premium account		25
General reserve		30
Purchases	790	
Profit at 1/7/04		17
Sales returns	33	
Purchases returns		25
Administration salaries	150	
Workshop wages	62	
Workshop machinery	175	
Depreciation thereon at 1/7/04		65
Distribution and administration expenses	27	
Intangible assets	49	
Carriage outwards	8	
Inventory at 1/7/04	44	
Rent receivable		12
Ordinary share capital		400
Directors salaries	31	
Trade receivables	207	
Trade payables		69
Cash at bank	667	

The following adjustments (£'000) should be taken into account:

Inventory at 30/6/05 £66
Current tax due £19
Annual depreciation £15

Requirements
  (a) Prepare an Income Statement (expenses by function method) for 2004–
       05, in accordance with IAS 1 requirements.
  (b) Provide a commentary on the results for the year.

3   The Income Statement of Rienzi for the year ending 30 June 2005 and
Balance Sheets as at 30 June 2005 and 2004 were as follows:

Income Statement (£m)

Sales		1,440
Raw materials used	140	
Administration costs	188	
Depreciation	236	
		564
Operating profit		876
Interest payable		(56)
Profit before tax		820
Taxation		(248)
Profit for the year		572

Balance Sheets

	2004		2005	
Property plant and equipment				
Cost	3,192		3,120	
Depreciation	(636)	2,556	(448)	2,672
Current assets				
Inventory	48		40	
Trade receivables	152		116	
Bank	96	296	112	268
Total assets		2,852		2,940

Equity and liabilities
Capital and reserves

Share capital	720		680	
Share premium	72		48	
Retained earnings	1,432	2,224	1,028	1,756

Non-current liabilities

Loans		400		1,000

Current liabilities

Trade payables	24		12	
Taxation	204	228	172	184
		2,852		2,940

During the year, a new drilling machine cost £72,000.

Requirements
(a) Prepare a cash flow statement for the year ended 30 June 2005, on the IAS 7 indirect method.
(b) Provide a brief commentary on the results for the year.

4 Your new company chairman has approached you as Director of Finance. He is quite happy with the structure and contents of an Income Statement and a Balance Sheet, but is less certain about a Statement of Changes in Equity and a Statement of Recognised Income and Expense.

Requirements
Draft a formal note to your Chairman, explaining, in non-technical language, the main structure and purpose of each document, that he might use at the forthcoming Annual General Meeting.

5 Lohengrin plc has produced the following financial statements for its two most recent financial years, ending on 31 December:

Income Statement	20X2 (£'000)	20X3 (£'000)
Sales	16,200	19,500
Cost of sales	10,400	10,950
Gross profit	5,800	8,550
Other expenses	(1,100)	(2,500)
Interest payable	(250)	(500)
Net profit	4,450	5,550
Dividends paid in year	600	700

Balance Sheets

Non-current assets (net)		3,000		5,450
Current assets				
Inventories	900		900	
Trade receivables	1,850		2,950	
Cash	1,200	3,950	1,400	5,250
		6,950		10,700
Capital and reserves				
Share capital		2,000		2,000
Revaluation reserve		800		1,850
Retained profit		1,330		3,900
		4,130		7,750
Long-term liabilities				
12% loan		2,000		2,000
Current liabilities				
Trade payables		820		950
		6,950		10,700

Requirements
(a) Calculate eight performance ratios for each year and on the basis of these results.
(b) briefly give reasons for either investing or not investing in the company.

6 Tristan Ltd currently allows trade customers 90 days in which to pay. Its annual sales are £3 million and its bad debts are 4% of that figure. In an attempt to reduce this revenue loss, it is proposing to reduce the credit period to 30 days. Tristan expects the consequences of this to be a reduction of bad debts to 1% of turnover, but a reduction of 25% in sales. There will be a similar impact in quantity of purchases and inventory holdings.

Current relevant figures are: Inventory £650, 000: Annual purchases £400, 000: Payables £60, 000.

Requirements
Given a 10% cost of capital, what is the likely impact of this proposal on Tristan's annual financing cost.

7   Write short notes on

(a)   the danger of over reliance on trade credit as a source of finance and

(b)   the proposal that a significant quantity of finished product inventory is good for a company.

8   Isolde plc has consulted you about the length of the company's trade/ operating cycle. The following figures, (in £'000), have been provided for the past 3 years:

	2004	2005	2006
Inventory of raw materials	75	80	100
Inventory of finished goods	200	220	270
Raw material purchases	790	830	880
Cost of sales	1,500	1,550	1,680
Trade receivables	160	200	310
Trade payables	120	150	170
Sales	1,800	1,900	2,330

Requirements

(a)   Calculate the length of Isolde's trade/operating cycle for the two most recent years.

(b)   Comment on what your calculations reveal.

Solutions to Revision Questions

1 (a) The four general purpose statements, mentioned in guidance accompanying IAS 1 are the Income Statement, Balance Sheet, Statement of Changes in Equity and a Statement of Recognised Income and Expense (see Appendix C). The guidance is not intended to show a complete set of financial statements. There is no exhibit for a Cash Flow Statement (dealt with in IAS 7), a summary of significant accounting policies, or other explanatory Notes to the accounts.

The guidance also comments, in respect of the four statements, that they are merely examples of ways in which minimum reporting standards might be presented. Other formats may be equally appropriate. The statements are shown in Appendix C of this book and these may be regarded as depicting the minimum disclosures to be made on the face of financial statements. Comparative figures are required for all items, unless specifically not required by an Accounting Standard.

(b) The IAS 1 guidance heading "Notes" indicates what should be provided (see page 203).

2 (a) Tannhauser plc

Income Statement for the year ended 30 June 2005 (£'000)

Sales revenue		1,567
Inventory increase (goods for sale)		22
		1,589
Purchase of goods for resale (790−25)		765
		824
Staff costs (150+62)	212	
Depreciation	15	
Other operating charges (8+27+31)	66	293
Profit from operations		531
Rent income		12
		543
Taxation		(19)
Profit for year		**524**

(b) A commentary on these results would be very difficult, given the absence of any comparative figures, a Balance Sheet or other assistance. Certainly, having regard to the accounting profit b/f at 1/7/04, the 2004–05 profit of

£524,000, seems very healthy. There is, however, no indication of how this profit has been distributed. All of this reinforces a key exam. point in a question dealing with a "commentary on results". This is that you can never have enough information. In this case, at least, the previous years comparatives for both the Income Statement and the Balance Sheet, would enable some sort of results review to be attempted.

3   Rienzi

Cash Flow Statement for the year ended 30 June 2005 (£'000)

Operating activities		
Profit before tax	820	
Depreciation*	188	
Interest paid	56	
Inventory increase	(8)	
Receivables increase	(36)	
Payables increase	12	
	1,032	
Interest paid	(56)	
Dividends paid	(168)	
Tax paid	(216)	
Operating activities cash flow		592
Acquisition of new machine		(72)
		520
Share capital issued	64	
Loans repaid	(600)	(536)
Decrease in cash		(16)
Cash at beginning of year		112
Cash at end of year		96

* Depreciation in year 236–48 (disposal). If in doubt, construct a T account!

4   An important exam point here is the word "formal". Thus, the back of an envelope job is not acceptable, apart from which you may wish to make a good impression on your new Chairman The qualities of a good report will therefore be required, with the usual "topping and tailing", and a well-structured and presented set of comments in between.

The explanations that might be included in your formal note for the Equity Statement are that it reconciles changes in the financial position of an organisation, so far as sums due to the owners are concerned. It therefore lists opening and closing balances relating to share capital and each class of reserve, with an analysis of movements on each heading during the year. An example is given in Appendix C. It was formerly called a Reconciliation of Movements in Shareholders Funds (a requirement under FRS 3)

The Statement of Recognised Income and Expense, is an alternative way of presenting information about changes in equity. An example of the structure is shown in page 000.

5   Lohengrin performance ratios

The choice of which ratios to select in this question is left entirely to you, In this circumstance, it is advisable to produce a range of ratios, covering the main traditional categories (profitability, liquidity, efficiency, gearing and investor). This is to show the examiner the breadth of your knowledge!). Such choice, of course, will also be governed by the amount of material available.

	20X2		20X3	
Gross profit margin	5,800/16,200	35.8%	8,550/19,500	43.8%
Net profit margin	4,450/16,200	27.5%	5,550/19,200	28.9%
ROCE	4,700/6,130	76.6%	6,050/9,750	62.0%
Acid test (Quick)	3,050/820	3.7:1	3,350/950	3.5:1
Asset turnover	16,200/6,130	2.6 times	19,500/9,750	2.0 times
Stock turnover	900/10,400 × 365	31.5 days	2,000/10,950 × 365	66.6 days
Gearing	2,000/6,130	32.6%	2,000/9,750	20.5%

A brief review of each chosen ratio shows:

GPM – a very healthy increase.
NPM – an 8.3% increase, but one which is out of line with the GPM movement; review level of expenditures.
ROCE – a significant reduction, which may be due to big increases in reserves or retained profits.
Acid Test – very much the same, but with cash reserves well able to meet trade payables – a very healthy liquidity position.

Financial Accounting and Reporting

Asset Turnover – the extent to which assets are being managed to generate profits has worsened significantly.This may be due to competition, but we don't really know.

Stock Turnover – with no increase in inventories, this big increase may suggest a need for a thorough look at ways of increasing trade, perhaps by reviewing credit terms.

Gearing – both are well within traditional low gearing bounds (under 50%).

OVERALL THOUGHT – on the basis of what we have available, Lohengrin would be worth a modest investment.

6 Tristan

Current level of receivables:

£3m × 90/365 = £780,000

New level of receivables: £3m × 75% × 30/365 = £184,500

Current financing requirement:

(650,000 + 780,000) − 60,000 = £1,370,000

New financing requirement (487,500 + 184,500) − 45,000 = £627,000

Thus the change in the financing requirement is £1370,000 − 627,000 = 743,000 at 10% = £74,300.

7 (a) Terms of trade

In dealing with the management of short-term financing requirements of a business, two main types of credit will be met. Consumer Credit, which is offered to household customers and Trade Credit, which is issued by one business to another. If a company's terms of trade require payment within one month, that is, effectively, giving 30 days in which to pay. The absence of this cash in the bank involves a cost (loss of investment interest or a saving of overdraft interest), that must be met. The other side of that particular coin is that it may be a significant way in which to attract/retain customers. It is a matter of striking a balance between the two.

Trade credit from suppliers, is especially of value to new, small or growing firms. It is a valuable source of short-term finance, as a prop to day-to-day working capital. Since interest is rarely charged, it can also be a cheap source of finance, but if advantage is not taken of an early payment discount, then there is a cost factor. Over reliance may store up problems of cash flow and the acquiring of a bad trade reputation. If a business is over reliant on extended credit from one supplier, then future supplies of raw material may not be easy to obtain. Such a policy may, in addition, worsen a company's credit rating, which could result in future additional credit being difficult to obtain.

(b) A significant quantity of finished goods, may act as a very useful buffer to iron out peaks and troughs of production. Customers should be able to always obtain goods as required. This will generate a good name for prompt and efficient service. Such inventories do however, have big cost disadvantages. Much capital is tied up in stocks, which have to be stored, secured and insured. As Section F of Chapter 1 shows, modern production methods are moving away from "make and store until required", to a much leaner JIT approach.

8   Isolde

The length of the trading cycle may be calculated as follows:

$$\frac{\text{Average raw materials}}{\text{Purchases}} + \frac{\text{Average finished goods}}{\text{Cost of sales}} + \frac{\text{Average Receivables}}{\text{Sales}}$$

$$- \frac{\text{Average Payables}}{\text{Purchases}}$$

This gives the following calculations. For 2004–05, $(77.5/830) + (210/1550) + (180/1900) - (135/830)$. All multiplied by 365, i.e. $34 + 49 + 35 - 59 = 59$ days.

For 2005–06, the figures are $(90/880) + (245/1,680) + (255/2,330) - (160/880)$. All multiplied by 365 in $37 + 15 + 40 - 66 = 26$ days.

A reduction of 33 days 56% and thus a most creditable performance!

Auditing and Governance

There will be a time to audit the accounts later

(Louis Macneice)

A   Introduction

Auditing is a specialised area of financial administration, with its own professional body, International Auditing Standards and many statutory requirements, particularly those contained in the Companies Acts of 1985, 1989 and 2006. In the United Kingdom, regulation of the work of auditors is within the remit of the Auditing Practices Board (APB), under the general umbrella of the Financial Reporting Council. Internationally, auditing is regulated by the International Auditing and Assurance Standards Board, through the issues of ISAs (International Standards on Auditing)

It does not, however, figure extensively in the CIMA examination syllabus, since in real life, the majority of Company audit work is the responsibility of members of the ICA or CACA. These professional accountancy bodies become "Recognised Supervisory Bodies" for this purpose. Indeed, members of CIMA and CIPFA are not allowed, by law, to audit and give an Opinion on the accounts of companies.

Having said all that, auditing is such an important aspect of financial management, that a knowledge of the structure and basics are essential for the skills of a qualified management accountant.

In one way or another, auditing affects most people in the daily round. The stewardship of bodies in which the public invests is in the hands of appointed directors, but is subject to detailed scrutiny by the annual audit process. That basic statutory requirement has been given added impetus in recent years with the growth of what is now generically termed "corporate governance", of which there is more later on in this chapter. Both corporate governance and auditing have been very much in the recent public eye, as the result of several large-scale company frauds, to the detriment of stakeholders. There is no specific reference to corporate governance in the P7 syllabus content, but reference to recent major financial scandals later in this chapter and subsequent corrective action by authorities have highlighted the subject. The attitude and behaviour of directors of public companies have placed greater pressure both on the auditors to report on the truth and fairness of financial statements and on the directors to abide by a code of professional conduct (at present a non-statutory document).

B External Audit and the Reporting Process

The main sequential stages of the external audit of a business, might usefully be summarised as follows:

(i) *The Business Environment and Statute Law*:
Statutory requirements – legal rights, duties and liabilities of auditors – the appointment of auditors – United Kingdom and International Auditing Standards

(ii) *Planning the Audit*:
What is to be covered – past work and vulnerable areas – what risks may arise?

(iii) *Gathering Audit Evidence*:
Materiality – allocation of work in the audit team – sampling – the recording of evidence – audit files – confidentiality

(iv) *Forming an Opinion*:
Has the audit been wide enough? – Is more work required? – an independent scrutiny of what has been done by the audit partner responsible

(v) *The Audit Report*:
Drafting the Statutory Report – what type of Report matches the evidence gathered – the internal Management Letter

Requirements of CIMA Paper P7

This is the only paper at Managerial Level that examines auditing in any depth, though clearly, auditing knowledge is useful as a general background in studying other papers. The P7 requirement is short and is contained within syllabus Part B, which makes up 10% of the syllabus. At Learning Outcome (vii) of Part B, it states that students should be able to "explain in general terms, the role of the external auditor, the elements of the Audit Report and types of qualification of that Report".

The syllabus content relating to auditing, states that the paper covers knowledge of "the powers and duties of the external auditors, the Audit Report and its qualification for accounting statements not in accordance with best practice". The risk and control aspects of auditing are also met in Paper P3 at strategic level.

Having set out the requirements of the CIMA examiners, students will now be introduced to more detail of each of the main stages of an external audit.

External Audit and the Reporting Process

Powers and duties of auditors

The statutory requirement for all companies to appoint an external auditor is contained in the Companies Acts of 1985 and 1989. The Companies Act 2006 also contains audit requirements. The Acts set out in detail, provisions relating to the appointment and resignation of auditors and their rights and duties. The statutes are supplemented by Auditing Standards, initially issued by the APB. In 2004, in order to support the international harmonisation of auditing Standards, the APB adopted the ISAs and the International Standard on Quality Control 1 (ISQC1), issued by the International Audit and Assurance Standards Board (IAASB).

As the exam requirements are clearly geared towards the external audit of the financial statements of a business, it is now appropriate to give the definition of an audit from a Glossary of Terms issued by the APB:

> An exercise whose objective is to enable auditors to express an opinion whether the financial statements give a true and fair view... of the entity's affairs at the period end and of its profit or loss (or income and expenditure) for the period then ended and have been properly prepared in accordance with the applicable reporting framework (e.g. relevant legislation and applicable accounting standards)

In February 1996, the APB published its nine fundamental principles of Independent Auditing. These principles and the APB comment on each are set out below. They are well worth reading, as each principle sets out a key requirement essential to an auditors work in providing an independent report on the financial statements of a business.

APB fundamental principles of Independent Auditing

Principle	APB comment
1 Accountability	Auditors act in the interests of primary stakeholders, whilst having regard to the wider public interest.
	The identity of primary stakeholders is determined by reference to the statute or agreement requiring an audit: in the case of companies the primary stakeholder is the general body of shareholders.

Principle	APB comment
2 Integrity	Auditors act with integrity, fulfilling their responsibilities with honesty, fairness and truthfulness.
	Confidential information obtained in the course of the audit is disclosed only when required in the public interest, or by operation of law.
3 Objectivity and Independence	Auditors are objective.
	They express opinions independently of the entity and its directors.
4 Competence	Auditors act with professional skill, derived from their qualification, training and practical experience.
	This demands an understanding of financial reporting and business issues, together with expertise in accumulating and assessing the evidence necessary to form an opinion.
5 Rigour	Auditors approach their work with thoroughness and with an attitude of professional scepticism.
	They assess critically the information and explanations obtained in the course of their work and such additional evidence as they consider necessary for the purposes of their audit.
6 Judgement	Auditors apply professional judgement taking account of materiality in the context of the matters on which they are reporting.
7 Clear communication	Auditors' reports contain clear expressions of opinion and set out information necessary for a proper understanding of that opinion.
8 Association	Auditors allow their reports to be included in documents containing other information only if they consider that the additional information is not in conflict with the matters covered by their report and they have no cause to believe it to be misleading.
9 Providing value	Auditors add to the reliability and quality of financial reporting; they provide to directors and officers constructive observations arising from the audit process; and thereby contribute to the effective operation of business, capital markets and the public sector.

Published in February 1996 by the Auditing Practices Board

An example of the contents of such a Report is set out below. This is an example of an "unqualified" report, where there are no matters to be drawn to the attention of shareholders. The requirements and Report wording, where there are such matters, are dealt with later in this chapter.

Independent auditors' report to the members of ABC plc

We have audited the group and parent company financial statements (the "financial statements") of ABC plc for the year ended 31 December 2006 which comprise the group income statements, the group and parent company balance sheets, the group and parent company cash flow statements, the group and parent company statements of change in shareholders' equity and the related notes. These financial statements have been prepared under the accounting policies set out therein. We have also audited the information in the directors' remuneration report that is described as having been audited.

Respective responsibilities of directors and auditors

The directors' responsibilities for preparing the annual report, the directors' remuneration report and the financial statements in accordance with applicable law and International Financial Reporting Standards (IFRSs) as adopted by the European Union are set out in the statement of directors' responsibilities.

Our responsibility is to audit the financial statements and the part of the directors' remuneration report to be audited in accordance with relevant legal and regulatory requirements and International Standards on Auditing (UK and Ireland). This report, including the opinion, has been prepared for and only for the company's members as a body in accordance with Section 235 of the Companies Act 1985 and for no other purpose. We do not, in giving this opinion, accept or assume responsibility for any other purpose or to any other person to whom this report is shown or into whose hands it may come save where expressly agreed by our prior consent in writing.

We report to you our opinion as to whether the financial statements give a true and fair view and whether the financial statements and the part of the directors' remuneration report to be audited have been properly prepared in accordance with the Companies Act 1985 and Article 4 of the IAS Regulation. We also report to you whether in our opinion the information given in the directors' report is consistent with the financial statements. We also report to you if, in our opinion the company has not kept proper accounting records, if we have not received all the information and explanations we require for our audit, or if information specified by law regarding directors' remuneration and other transactions is not disclosed.

We review whether the corporate governance statement reflects the company's compliance with the nine provisions of the (2003 FRC Combined Code) speci- fied for our review by the Listing Rules of the Financial Services Authority, and we report if it does not. We are not required to consider whether the board's statements on internal control cover all risks and controls, or form an opinion on the effectiveness of the group's corporate governance procedures or its risk and control procedures.

We read other information contained in the annual report and consider whether it is consistent with the audited financial statements. The other information comprises only the directors' report, the unaudited part of the directors' remu- neration report, the chairman's statement, the operating and financial review and the corporate governance statement. We consider the implications for our report if we become aware of any apparent misstatements or material incon- sistencies with the financial statements. Our responsibilities do not extend to any other information.

Basis of Audit Opinion

We conducted our audit in accordance with International Standards on Audit- ing (UK and Ireland) issued by the APB. An audit includes examination, on a test basis, of evidence relevant to the amounts and disclosures in the financial statements and the part of the directors' remuneration report to be audited. It also includes an assessment of the significant estimates and judgements made by the directors in the preparation of the financial statements, and of whether the accounting policies are appropriate to the group's and company's circumstances, consistently applied and adequately disclosed.

We planned and performed our audit so as to obtain all the information and explanations which we considered necessary in order to provide us with suf- ficient evidence to give reasonable assurance that the financial statements and the part of the directors' remuneration report to be audited are free from mate- rial misstatement, whether caused by fraud or other irregularity or error. In forming our opinion, we also evaluated the overall adequacy of the presenta- tion of information in the financial statements and the part of the directors' remuneration report to be audited.

Opinion

In our opinion:

- the financial statements give a true and fair view, in accordance with IFRSs as adopted by the European Union, of the state of the group's and the parent company's affairs as at 31 December 2006 and of its profit [loss] and cash flows for the year then ended;
- the financial statements and the part of the directors' remuneration report to be audited have been properly prepared in accordance with the Companies Act 1985 and Article 4 of the IAS Regulation; and
- the information given in the directors' report is consistent with the financial statements.

As explained in Note X, to the group financial statements the group in addition to complying with its legal obligations to comply with IFRSs as adopted by the European Union, has also complied with the IFRSs as issued by the International Accounting Standards Board.

In our opinion the group financial statements give a true and fair view, in accordance with IFRSs, of the state of the group's affairs as at 31 December 2006 and of its profit [loss] and cash flows for the year then ended.

> Tickett and Runne LLP
> Chartered Accountants and Registered Auditors
> Location
> Date

A further example, now shown, is of an independent auditor's Report on the summarised accounts of the HBOS for 2006.

Statement of the independent auditors' to the members of HBOS plc
(pursuant to Section 251 of the Companies Act 1985)

We have examined the Summary Consolidated Income Statement and Summary Consolidated Balance Sheet (together "the summary financial statement") set out on pages 16 and 17.

This statement is made solely to the Company's members, as a body, in accordance with section 251 of the Companies Act 1985. Our work has been undertaken so that we might state to the Company's members those matters we are required to state to them in such a statement and for no other purpose. To the fullest extent permitted by law, we do not accept or assume responsibility to anyone other than the Company and the Company's members as a body, for our work, for this statement, or for the opinions we have formed.

Respective responsibilities of directors and auditors

The directors are responsible for preparing the Annual Review & Summary Financial Statement in accordance with applicable United Kingdom law. Our responsibility is to report to you our opinion on the consistency of the summary financial statement within the Annual Review & Summary Financial Statement with the full annual accounts and the report to the Board in relation to remuneration policy and practice, and its compliance with the relevant requirements of section 251 of the Companies Act 1985 and the regulations made thereunder. We also read the other information contained in the Annual Review & Summary Financial Statement and consider the implications for our report if we become aware of any apparent misstatements or material inconsistencies with the summary financial statement.

Basis of Opinion

We conducted our work in accordance with Bulletin 1999/96 "The auditor's statement on the summary financial statement" issued by the Auditing Practices Board for use in the United Kingdom. Our report on the Group's full annual accounts describes the basis of our audit opinion on those accounts.

Opinion

In our opinion the summary financial statement is consistent with the full annual accounts, the directors' report and the report of the Board in relation to remuneration policy and practice of HBOS plc for the year ended 31 December 2006 and complies with the applicable requirements of section 251 of the Companies Act 1985 and the regulations made thereunder.

KPMG Audit Plc

Chartered Accountants, Registered Auditor, Edinburgh, 27 February 2007.

You will see that the final, Opinion, paragraphs place a considerable onus on the signature of the auditor. It is confirming that there are no significant ("material") errors in the published statements, that would mislead a reasonably competent reader. The auditor has to exercise his/her judgement on what is material. The consequences of giving an unqualified Opinion, which should have been qualified are very serious, leaving an auditor open to legal action under both civil and criminal law. So what work does the auditor carry out to enable the correct type of Opinion to be formed? A brief summary of the sequential steps will now follow.

Planning the audit

Given the nature of the company's business, the auditor should be aware of what could be wrong with the financial statements. The potential risks are thus indicated. The auditor should then see what systems and controls are in place to obviate these risks and then apply tests of control to see if they are working as they should, so as to prevent material misstatements.

The annual plan will require the auditor to be right up to date with the nature of the business (from previous audit papers, visits and discussions, press comment, trade magazines, etc.).

Decide which aspects of the business are to be especially looked at this year, and allocate that work between the grades of experience in the audit team.

Prepare detailed audit programmes to examine each selected aspect in detail sufficient to confirm that all appears to be well.

Gathering evidence

As there must be a choice of what is to be covered in the audit, be aware of the risks inherent in planning what to leave out of the detailed work. Plan to reduce these risks to a minimum.

1 Ensure that all evidence is promptly, adequately and confidentially recorded in the audit working papers.
2 Test individual systems by following transactions from beginning to end in the company's books
3 Seek such documents and oral explanations as may be required, from company staff.

Apply analytical procedures, i.e. do the figures look right when compared with other relevant figures and when seen as part of a trend?

Additional pre-opinion work

Following the completion of gathering the detailed evidence, and before starting to prepare Reports, the auditor must consider such important issues as, is the business a "going concern"?, any representations made by the management during the course of the audit, events subsequent to the Balance Sheet date and the existence of any potential future liabilities or contingencies. All of these may require amendments to the draft statements, or a reference in the Audit Report.

Respective responsibilities of directors and auditors

There is a clear division of responsibilities between the directors and auditors. This is reflected in the wording of the formal auditor's report. The management of an entity is charged with establishing the framework within which the company operates. This "control environment" establishes the overall attitude of "doing things properly and in accordance with laid down systems and procedures". Management is responsible for preparing and placing the annual financial statements before the auditors, asserting them to be correct. It is the auditor's task, as the result of the annual audit procedures to confirm that the statements give a "true and fair" view and to report if this is not the case. How this is done, will be seen in the next section.

Forming an Opinion

An appendix to ISA 700, considers the process of forming an Audit Opinion, using a Flowchart, below. The principal matters which auditors need to consider in forming an Opinion, may be expressed in the following questions:

1 Has all the information and necessary explanations, been obtained in accordance with the Plan?
2 Have all accounting and auditing Standards been followed?
3 Do the statements, as prepared by the directors, give a "true and fair view"?

Forming an opinion on financial statements

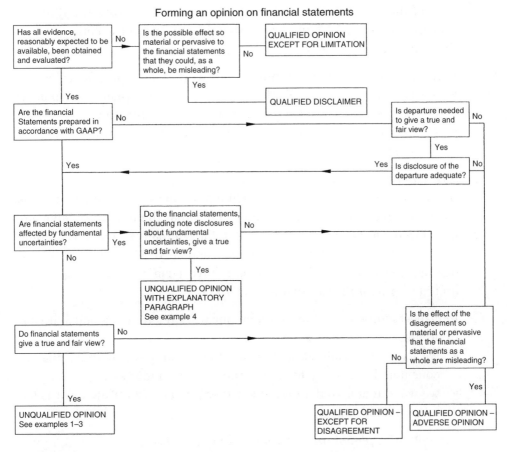

SAS 600 – Auditor's Reports on Financial Statements, Appendix 1

Types of audit report

An example of an "unqualified" Audit Report has already been seen. Modified Reports arise when auditors do not believe that they can state, without reservation, that the statements do give a "true and fair" view. There are three main circumstances in which this may be necessary and these are expressed by ISA 600, as follows:

1 *A Qualified Opinion*
   Except for any adjustments that might have been found to be necessary had we been able to obtain sufficient evidence concerning cash sales, in our opinion the financial statements give a true and fair view of the

state of the company's affairs as at (date) and of its profit (loss) for the year then ended and have been properly prepared in accordance with the Companies Act 1985.

In respect alone of the limitation on our work relating to cash sales:
- we have not obtained all the information and explanations that we considered necessary for the purpose of our audit; and
- we were unable to determine whether proper accounting records had been maintained

2   *A Disclaimer of Opinion*

Because of the possible effect of the limitation in evidence available to us, we are unable to form an opinion as to whether the financial statements give a true and fair view of the state of the company's affairs as at (date) or of its profit (loss) for the year then ended. In all other respects, in our opinion the financial statements have been properly prepared in accordance with the Companies Act 1985.

In respect alone of the limitation on our work relating to stock and work in progress:
- we have not obtained all the information and explanations that we considered necessary for the purpose of our audit; and
- we were unable to determine whether proper accounting records had been maintained

"Except for" Opinion arising from a limitation of scope

The example of an "except for" Opinion arising from a limitation of scope given in SAS 600 relates to the situation where there was a lack of control over a company's cash sales and hence the auditor could not rely on the system when verifying cash sales. In addition, the auditor was unable to find other evidence that could be used to verify such sales.

3   *An Adverse Opinion*

An example of an adverse Opinion is reproduced below. This example concerns a very significant failure by the company to apply a fundamental accounting concept – prudence. The circumstances are clear from the Opinion:

Adverse Opinion. as more fully explained in note . . . no provision has been made for losses expected to arise on certain long-term contracts currently in progress, as the directors consider that such losses should be offset against amounts recoverable on other long-term contracts. In our opinion, provision should be made for foreseeable losses on individual contracts as required by Statement of Standard Accounting Practice 9. If losses had been so recognised the effect would have been to reduce the profit before and after tax for the year and the contract work in progress at 31 December 19 by £...

In view of the effect of the failure to provide for the losses referred to above, in our opinion the financial statements do not give a true and fair view of the state of the company's affairs as at (date) and of its profit (loss) for the year then ended. In all other respects, in our opinion the financial statements have been properly prepared in accordance with the Companies Act 1985.

In any of these circumstances, the auditor is required to include substantive reasons in the Report and, unless impracticable, a quantification of the possible effects on the financial statements.

Let us now look at the circumstances in which each may be used:

Qualified   where the auditor concludes that the effect of any disagreement with management, or a limitation on the scope of the work performed is not so material and pervasive as to require a disclaimer or an adverse Opinion

Disclaimer   when the possible effect of a limitation on scope is so material and pervasive that insufficient audit evidence has been obtained to enable an Opinion to be expressed.

Adverse   where a disagreement with management is so material and pervasive that the auditor concludes that a qualification is just not adequate to disclose the misleading or incomplete nature of the financial statements

A limitation of scope may exist, e.g. where records are missing, or where questions are not answered.

At a meeting on 9 August 2005, the Financial Reporting Council published its analysis of the implications of the new international accounting and auditing standards on the principle of "true and fair view" and the responsibilities of auditors. The Council reported that the move to IASs will result in changes in key measures such as profit and net assets, the format of financial statements and the terminology used in preparing the statements. The FRC analysis looked particularly at the possible replacement of the "true and fair view" test, by a "fair presentation" requirement, that financial statements should satisfy.

The Council concluded that the true and fair view concept should remain the cornerstone of financial reporting and auditing in the United Kingdom. It felt that there had been no substantive change in the objectives of an audit and the nature of an auditor's responsibilities and that the need for professional judgement remains central to the work of preparers of accounts and auditors in the United Kingdom.

The Management Letter

In addition to the completion of the formal Audit Report and Opinion, auditors are required under ISA 260 to report to "those charged with the governance" of a business. A Management Letter is an informal and internal document, enabling the auditor to communicate matters which have come to their attention, during the audit and on which action may be required, e.g. adjustments to an accounting procedure. Such issues will no doubt be followed up as part of planning for the next formal audit. They are not yet matters which require to be mentioned in the formal Audit Report.

The Audit Committee

As part of the good corporate governance of a business, directors will have established an audit committee to exercise continuous and live oversight of systems and internal controls. This committee will receive and make recommendations on the reports of external auditors, deal with all audit matters and aid communications between the business and the auditor. New European Rules, issued early in 2007, tighten audit regulations, to reduce the risk of further major financial scandals.

These proposals, which are supported by the financial institutions of the City of London, strengthen the regulation of auditing firms that sign off accounts of companies listed on European stock markets. The Financial Reporting Council and the big accountancy firms remain concerned over the application of these new rules. The EU Directive, however, gives national regulators the power to force auditors of any company seeking to issue shares in Europe, to meet these new European standards.

The requirements of the Sarbanes–Oxley Act (see later in this chapter) and the Companies Act 2006, now require a much greater scrutiny role for members of an Audit Committee. The EU Directive lays heavy emphasis on the qualifications needed to chair a Committee, clarifies the duties of statutory auditors and provides for public oversight of the audit profession. There are also EU proposals to limit auditor liability throughout the EU. The Companies Act 2006 provides that companies and their auditors may now agree, privately, to limit an auditor's liability in relation to the company's accounts, negligence, default, breach of duty and breach of trust.

C   Internal Audit

The work of the external auditor may be regarded as "completed", in that the main audit takes place annually over, say a 4-week period, when the audit team visits the business. Of course, this does not mean that nothing happens for the remaining weeks of the year. Many factors, not least trust and confidence, will determine what contact takes place in "non-audit" weeks. Throughout the year, the auditor will regularly liaise with management and receive relevant reports and documents.

The extent of both this contact and of the annual audit itself, might be governed by the existence of an internal audit function within the business. The internal audit will thus be a continuous and detailed appraisal of financial processes. A good internal audit section may well reduce the time and cost devoted to the annual external audit and keep management on its toes.

There is no statutory requirement for internal audit (except for local authorities and National Health Service bodies), but many larger companies will have staff dedicated to continuous internal reviews, or buy in such expertise. The Institute of Internal Auditors issued, in 1991, a statement which defined internal audit as "an independent appraisal function to examine and evaluate its activities as a service to the organisation and to help staff discharge their responsibilities effectively". As with external audit, a key word here is "independent," which may be difficult to achieve, as internal audit staff will be on the company's payroll.

D   Corporate Governance and the Combined Code

These subjects are not referred to in the Paper P7 syllabus, but they have assumed increasing importance in recent years, for the brief reasons given at the beginning of this chapter. They will be dealt with in a little more detail here, especially as CIMA made important changes to its Certificate in Business

Accounting syllabus from November 2006. Paper CO5 was extended from Business Law to include both Ethics and Corporate Governance. Thus, students coming to Paper P7 from AAT, may not have met these important aspects of modern day business.

A flavour of what is involved can be obtained from the CIMA syllabus for CO5, which covers:

1 The role and key objectives of corporate governance in relation to ethics and the law.
2 Development of corporate governance internationally.
3 The behaviour of directors in relation to corporate governance and duty of care towards their stakeholders.
4 The role of the company board in establishing corporate governance standards.
5 Types of board structures and corporate governance issues.
6 Policies and procedures for "best practice" companies.
7 Rules and principles based approaches to governance.
8 The regulatory governance framework.

Corporate governance has been defined as "the exercise of power over and responsibility for, corporate entities". It is thus concerned with the manner in which directors carry out their stewardship responsibilities. Directors are appointed to act in the best interest of their shareholders and to assist them towards this goal, the Combined Code on Corporate Governance has been developed in recent years.

The Code was issued by the Financial Reporting Council in 2003, in response to public concerns about the actions and motivation of some company directors in relation to their stewardship duties on behalf of all stakeholders of a company. The Code is a set of guidelines which can be used to determine whether the directors have carried out their duties adequately, in an appropriate manner and in the best interests of the shareholders they represent. The FRC recently sought the views of a wide range of interested parties on the effectiveness and relevance of the Code to the improvement of board performance.

Development of the Code began with the Cadbury Report in May 1991. In essence, this required directors to state in the published accounts, how they had met the requirements of a nationally published code of practice and, if not, to say why. In July 1993 the Greenbury Report looked specifically at the remuneration and rewards of directors.

Both of these Reports were then reviewed together by Sir Ronald Hampel (former Chairman of ICI plc) and from this review came, in June 1998, the first version of the Combined Code. The Code has been updated several times since then, as the result of the work of further committees looking at specific aspects of the broad subject. These were the Turnbull Report on Internal Controls (2002–03), the Smith Guidance on Audit Committees (2003) and the Higgs Report on the role and effectiveness of executive directors (also in 2003).

The International Federation of Accountants (IFAC), reviewed the working of the Code in 2004, by looking at performance in a mixture of 27 successful and failed companies. The major key failing was related to the culture and tone at the top of the company. A failure to set good examples and to uphold high ethical standards, resulted in the creation of unacceptable standards of behaviour, even to the extent of fraudulent practices, throughout the organisation.

The complete, updated Combined Code can be found on the Internet and downloaded therefrom. In addition, it is well worth looking at the corporate governance section of a company's annual report. The most illuminating recent commentary on what the Code has achieved appeared in *The Times* on 2 January 2007. A review of Britain's larger companies found that 40% of their chairmen or chief executives, felt that the Higgs recommendations had had no beneficial effect.

A Summary Corporate Governance Report (from the 2006 HBOS Annual Report and Accounts)

HBOS places a high degree of importance on how it conducts its business. Good corporate governance enables authority and accountability to be spread appropriately across the Group. In short, we believe that it makes us better at what we do.

HBOS Board of Directors

The Board met 10 times in 2006 and is legally responsible for running the Company on your behalf. Certain key decisions can only be made by the Board.

Non-executive Directors bring experience from the outside business world and an independent point of view to the Board's discussions. They represent a majority on the Board and a key part of the Chairman's job is to leverage their experience to maximum advantage.

The roles of Chairman and the Chief Executive are separate. The Chief Executive is responsible for running the Group's business and the Chairman (jointly with the Chief Executive) for developing the Group's strategy, overseeing its implementation and performance delivery as well as Board leadership.

Board Committees

The Board is supported by a structure of committees, including:

Remuneration Committee dealing with remuneration policy and practice for Directors and senior executives. Its members are all Non-executive Directors.

Nomination Committee which identifies suitable people to serve on the Board or as senior executives.

Most members are Non-executive Directors, plus the Chairman and the Chief Executive.

Audit Committee which reviews the Group's accounts, the risks the Group faces, 'whistleblowing' arrangements and internal controls. It also monitors the external auditors' independence and internal auditors' effectiveness. Divisional Risk Control Committees support the Audit Committee's work. One audit committee member is an external appointment, several are financial experts and all are considered independent.

Combined Code

A detailed report on corporate governance at HBOS plc, including the UK Listing Authority's Combined Code, is contained in the Annual Report and Accounts.

E Corporate Failures

A book review in the May 2007 edition of the CIMA magazine listed some of the more spectacular company collapses due to greed and corporate failure. It concluded that these frauds and the false accounting behind them were generally mechanisms for hiding greater and more widespread failings in the firms concerned.

A brief review of five recent collapses, or major financial scandals, is given below, to give an indication of what can go wrong if there is not an acceptable boardroom environment, adequate leadership or robust internal controls.

Pergamon Publishing

This media empire was built up in the 1970s by Robert Maxwell, who spent lavishly on acquisitions which included the publishers MacMillan and the *Daily Mirror*. Maxwell who had a reputation as a boardroom bully, drowned in November 1991 after which it was found that hundreds of millions of pounds had been siphoned off from Mirror Group pension funds, to prop up his ailing companies. Very many employees lost the funds set aside for their retirements.

Enron

Enron grew, in just 15 years from nothing to become the seventh largest US company, but its success turned out to involve an elaborate and massive scam, based on the false recording of turnover and the concealment of debts in offshore companies. Key officers were deeply involved and after the collapse, which ruined the lives of very many employees, were all jailed for long periods.

Parmalat

Based in Milan, Parmalat was the leading global company in the production of UHT milk. At the end of 2003, an 8 billion euro hole was discovered in the accounts. The founder, Calisto Tanzi, was jailed and admitted that he had diverted Parmalat funds into family businesses and one of Italy's leading soccer teams. Italians were shocked that such a vast and long established empire collapsed so quickly. In June 2007, four of the world's leading investment banks were ordered by a Milan judge, to stand trial for alleged wrongdoing in connection with the company.

Hollinger

One of North America's leading newspaper empires, Hollinger hit the head-lines in 2006–07, when its Chairman, Lord Black of Crossharbour and three associates were accused and charged with looting £60 million from the company in perks and bogus arrangements. Black himself faced 13 charges of fraud, racketeering and money laundering. A key aspect of this case, was "what was the Board told?" The trials began in Chicago in May 2007. Black was convicted on four counts on 13 July 2007.

McAlpine Slate

A very recent (2007) UK scandal at Alfred McAlpine, resulted in the dismissal of six executives, the resignation of the group Finance Director, a £56 million balance sheet provision and the involvement of the North Wales police. The alleged fraud was extensive, systematic and long running. Over a number of years, financial controls were systematically circumvented to overstate revenues. The company agreed that "the behaviour and collusion of the managers responsible was deliberate and involved fraud". Financial controls throughout the Group have since been "overhauled".

F   The Sarbanes–Oxley Act

This Act (often referred to as SARBOX or just SOX), was passed by the United States Congress in January 2002, in the wake of the Enron, Tyco and World.Com financial scandals. It purports to be an Act to protect investors "by improving the accuracy and reliability of corporate disclosures made pursuant to the securities laws and for other purposes".

Whilst this is an American Act, it essentially covers all UK companies that have or could have, contact with America. It brings onerous new governance rules both for company directors and company auditors. The requirements of the Act are best summarised in the CIMA *Official Terminology*, as follows:

> Section 404 of the Act: Management Assessment of Internal Controls, requires each annual report of an issuer to contain an internal control report, which should:
>
> (i)   State the responsibility of management for establishing and maintaining an adequate internal control structure and procedures for financial reporting; and
> (ii) Contain an assessment, as at the end of the issuer's fiscal year, of the effectiveness of the internal control structure and procedures of the issuer for financial reporting

These internal reports are subject to audit and revised US Auditing Standard 2 seeks to keep the auditor independent, while ensuring that the best interests of investors are upheld, through a thorough audit of internal controls. Latest developments in this area are contained in Chapter 2.

An excellent summary of the practical requirements of the Act and written by Michael Holt, has been published by Elsevier in its "CIMA Publishing" series.

Revision Questions

1 What do you understand by the term "stewardship"? How do directors of companies show good stewardship?
2 What specific purposes are served by:
   (a) The Audit Report?
   (b) The Management Letter?
3 From where do auditors obtain their powers and responsibilities?
4 How might internal and external auditors work together to the benefit of the business?
5 As part of evidence gathering, auditors may seek confirmatory evidence of transactions from outside of the business. Give SIX examples where this might be done.
6 Define the following audit terms:
   (a) True and Fair View
   (b) An Opinion
   (c) Going Concern
   (d) Disclaimer of Opinion
   (e) Independence of Audit
7 The "Control Environment" is of great importance in securing efficient financial administration in a business. Comment on THREE aspects that make up this environment.
8 Should auditors make their annual audit plan available to the top management of a company?

Solutions to Revision Questions

1   Stewardship may be defined as the competent management of another's property and as such, is a basic duty of a company director. Good stewardship in an organisation may be exemplified by having the right structure and atmosphere, with good, well published and up to date, rules and systems that are critically reviewed when things go wrong. An acid test of good stewardship is a clear annual audit Opinion, as a sign of reliable and relevant financial information.

2   (a) The audit report is a formal and independent annual confirmation to shareholders on the quality of the director's stewardship. It confirms that what is published in the financial statements gives a true and fair view of profit or loss for the review period and of the state of affairs at the balance sheet date. It confirms that the published accounts follow all statutory or other requirements, unless explicitly stated.

(b) This is a private letter to the company's management, following the annual audit. It lists possible improvements to systems and procedures and may offer advice or guidance on possible improvements or benefits.

3   Powers and responsibilities come directly from the Companies Acts of 1985 and 1989 and indirectly from auditing standards, issued by the APB. The APB also issues Practice Notes for specific areas or industries and Bulletins, where guidance is required on new and/or emerging topical issues.

Statutory duties are centred around a responsibility to perform a competent audit (a "duty of care") for the client company. An auditor's main rights include access to company records and oral explanations, as required; the right to attend company meetings and to be heard thereat.

4
  (i)   Through the exchange of discussed annual programmes of work and relevant reports prepared during the year.
 (ii)   By agreement on specific areas to be looked at by internal audit (perhaps following up suggestions in the last Management Letter).
(iii)   Regular meetings to discuss emerging matters relating to the development of the business, or within the industry sector generally.

5
  (i)   Writing to debtors (circularisation), to seek confirmation of the truth and accuracy of balances on personal accounts.
 (ii)   Seeking similar types of assurance and confirmation from creditors.

(iii) Physical examination of non-current assets to confirm the legitimacy of Balance Sheet or insurance values.

(iv) Acting as a customer, by personal inspection of a business' procedures (e.g. the ordering and cash payment for those goods).

(v) Seeking confirmation of investment holdings directly from the company concerned.

(vi) Obtaining direct evidence of asset ownership, by Land Registry enquiries and by contact with the lessor of leased assets.

6 (a) There is no legal definition of this final test of the quality of published financial statements. A practical definition can be found in Appendix A.

(b) An auditor's view that financial statements have been consistently prepared in accordance with relevant law and best practice (e.g Standards) and adequately disclose information sufficient for a proper understanding thereof.

(c) One of the original four fundamental concepts in SSAP2 and now a key feature of IAS 1. The assumption is that a business will continue for the foreseeable future without the necessity or intention to liquidate or significantly curtail the present scale of operations (thus damaging profits). A business that is not a going concern may publish a false Balance Sheet, since asset values shown therein may not be achieved in the event of liquidation.

(d) An auditor's statement to say what he/she has not been able to do in the annual audit, as the result of insufficient evidence to support an Opinion.

(e) An important principle of auditing is that auditors must and must be seen to be, independent so as to offer objective and impartial advice and judgements. Threats to perceived independence are an over reliance on a company's fees, family relationships, hospitality offered by the client company. Recognised Supervisory Bodies (see Appendix A) give clear guidance to deal with and ensure independence.

7 A satisfactory "control environment" stems from the attitude of the Board of Directors, but also involves the competence and integrity of all employees. Directors and senior managers lead by example, with a clear concentration on written codes of procedures and conduct; annual appraisals and discipline standards that are well known and rigorously followed. Three example of this in practice are the existence of an approved structure related to long-term objective; appropriate levels of delegation and personal accountability and good internal check (whereby too much power is concentrated in a single pair of hands).

8   In principle, this should be acceptable. The company needs to be able to produce the relevant documentation and personnel appropriate to the auditor looking at specific areas of the business. There would be little point in the auditor undertaking a major review of a company's treasury management department, if the accountable staff were out of the country for the whole of the audit period. There needs to be a balance between confidentiality and availability and much of this degree of balance will be governed by past performance and mutual trust.

Business Mathematics

Mathematics, rightly viewed, possesses ... – a beauty cold and austere, like that of a sculpture

(Bertrand Russell)

Introduction

This chapter considers five topics, specific in themselves but all having an important part to play in the practicalities of management accounting. Of the five subject chapters in this book, mathematics seems to cause the most angst among students, which is worrying given the importance of numeracy skills to an accountant.

It is certainly true that some good basic knowledge of mathematics can assist the accountant in the speed and accuracy of decision making and the solution of problems.

Those students who come best prepared to handle maths at Managerial Level, are those who have tackled *Fundamentals of Business Mathematics*, Paper CO3, at CBA level. That syllabus has the following topics:

A   Basic Mathematics
B   Probability
C   Summarising and Analysing Data
D   Inter-relationships between Variables
E   Forecasting
F   Financial Mathematics
G   Spreadsheets

Items A–F each carry a study weighting of 15% with spreadsheet preparation taking the balance of 10%.

This spread of knowledge confirms that these topics can and do occur regularly throughout each of CIMA's Professional Examination level papers. At Managerial Level, pretty well all of them impact on Papers P1 and P4, though Papers P7 and P8 are affected to a lesser extent.

The problem with this chapter is, therefore, how much to put in! One recommendation that, from experience can be strongly made, is to get hold of and study the expertly written Elsevier Learning System for Paper CO3. Another option, which I have actioned at a Further Education College, is to run a

5–6-week part-time course (say, 3 hours per week) in Business Mathematics before Managerial Level studies begin in earnest.

Either option will take more of your time, but in the totality of CIMA studying and your subsequent career, that will be entirely beneficial. Good mathematical knowledge is essential to examination success.

This book will therefore concentrate on the main concepts and techniques required in Papers P1, P2, P7 and P8. The two other Managerial Level Papers, P4 and P5 do not contain any specific references to business mathematics, but by implication (e.g. "Control of cost through professional management systems"), some mathematical knowledge will, no doubt, be required, or be advantageous in the examination room.

Back to Basics

So that we can move on to the more significant aspects of the subject and despite what has already been said, there is now an opportunity to test if you understand some basic calculations. The following 12 questions should be attempted without looking at the answers which follow!

Questions

1 $^7/_{12}$ as a fraction is what as a decimal?
2 Express 161.42375 correct to:
   (a) two decimal places
   (b) four decimal places
3 Multiply $(16 + 2)(22 - 2):6 + 9 \times 15$
4 What is the value of $5^{-6}: 8^2 \times 8^{-2}:16^{-5} \div 16^{-3}$
5 What is the reciprocal of 56?
6 Your salary is £42,000 after a 6% pay rise. What was it before?
7 The total cost of a product is £1200. What is the selling price on a margin of 25%?
8 Divide £70,000 in the ratio 350:840:49
9 Express 1.750 as a fraction
10 Calculate $\quad 6^{-1}:(16.2)^5 \times (16.2)^{1/4}:1^{15}$
    $$1^0:12^1$$
11 If annual sales of a product in year 1 (now) are £150,000, what will they be in year 6 if they are expected to increase by 20% compound annually?
12 The price of a product always keeps pace with the Retail Price Index. Ten years ago, when the RPI was 103.7, it cost £64.90. What is the cost today with an Index of 227? What is that as a percentage increase?

Answers

1 $^{7}/_{12} = 0.583$

2 (a) 161.42

   (b) 161.4238

3 $18 \times 20 = 360$ $6 + 135 = 141$ (see BODMAS in Appendix A)

4 $\dfrac{1}{5^6} = \dfrac{1}{15,625} : 8^{(2+(-2))} = 8^0 = 1 : 16^{-5-(-3)} = 16^{-2} = 1/16^2 = 1/256$

5 $1/56$

6 106% is £42,000, therefore, 100% is £39,623

7 If the margin is 25% ($^1/_4$) then the mark-up on the total cost is 1/5 or 20% = £400. Selling price is £1600

8 The shares are all exactly divisible by 7, so reduce them to LCD 50:120: $7 = 177$ shares, therefore, 1 share = £395.48 and the individual shares are = 19,774:47,458:2768

9 $1\dfrac{750}{1000} = 1\dfrac{75}{100} = 1\dfrac{3}{4}$

10 $\dfrac{1}{6} : (14.2)^4 \times (14.2)^{1/4} = (14.2)^{4.25} = 78,926.98 : 1 : 1 : 12$

11 £373,248

12 £142.07

A Algebra and Equations

Individual numbers are termed "integers", but if we use letters (like the x and y keys on a calculator) then we are dealing with "variables", which enable the calculation of values in numeric terms. Variables can be used to build up formulae.

Algebra comes from the Arabic, "al-jabr", literally, the reunion of broken parts, i.e. bonesetting. A more considered translation from the title of an Arabic book, is " the science of restoring what is missing and equating like with like". Thus, in this definition, an equation requires the maintenance of a balance between two quantities.

There are a couple of basic rules for solving equations which are as follows:

  (i) when you change sides, change the sign and

  (ii) what you do to one side of an equation must be immediately actioned on the other side

Examples of simple equations, (in each of these, we need to find the value of x)

(1) $x - 3 = 56$

$\qquad x = 56 + 3$ (3 changes sides and sign)

(2) $94x + 512 = 104x$

$\qquad 512 = 104x - 94x$

$\qquad 512 = 10x$

$\qquad 51.2 = x$

(3) $4\sqrt{x} + 32 = 40.6718$

$\qquad 4\sqrt{x} = 40.6718 - 32$ (change sides and sign)

$\qquad 4\sqrt{x} = 8.6718$

$\qquad \sqrt{x} = 2.16795$ (divide each side by 4)

$\qquad x = 4.7$ (square each side)

(4)   If $\dfrac{1}{3 + 12} = \dfrac{5}{4.9x - 2}$ What is the value of x?

$\qquad 3x + 12 = \dfrac{4.9x - 2}{5}$ (the reciprocal of each side)

$\qquad 15x + 60 = 4.9x - 2$ (multiplying by 5 on each side)

$\qquad 10.1x = -62$ (subtracting 4.9x and 60 from each side)

$\qquad x = -6.1386$

Simultaneous equations

Simultaneous equations are two, or more, equations, where the variables have the same values. They may be solved either graphically or algebraically.

Given the following equations, we need to calculate the values of x and y:

$$y = 3x + 16$$
$$2y = x + 72$$

An *algebraic* solution would give:

(1)   Multiply the second equation by 3 to get x the same:

$$y - 3x = 16$$
$$6y - 3x = 216$$

(2) With x cancelled out, we are left with:

$$5y = 200$$
$$y = 40$$

(3) Substituting the value of y in either equation (we use the second) enables the calculation of the value of x

$$2 \times 40 - x = 72$$
$$-x = 72 - 80 \quad \text{(or } 80 - 172 = x)$$
$$-x = -8$$
$$x = 8$$

A graphical solution to the problem would be presented as follows:

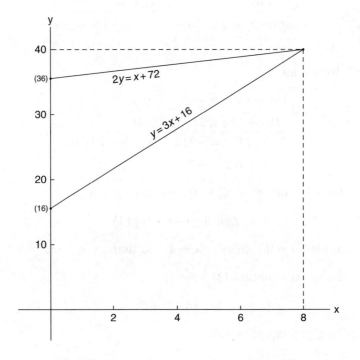

$y = 3x + 16$			$2y = x + 72$		
When	$x = 0$	$y = 16$	When	$x = 0$	$y = 36$
	2	22		2	37
	3	25		4	38
	4	28		6	39
	8	40		8	40

The final example below, is simultaneous equations with three unknowns. Here, you are required to find the values of x, y and z and show that you have checked your answers.

(1) $2x + 3y + 4z = 9$
(2) $3x - 2y - 3z = 3$
(3) $4x + 5y - 2z = 25$

multiply (1) by 3 $6x + 9y + 12z = 27$
multiply (2) by 2 $6x - 4y - 6z = 6$
subtract to give (4) $13y + 18z = 21$

multiply (1) by 2 $4x + 6y + 8z = 18$
(3) above $4x + 5y - 2z = 25$
subtract to give (5) $y + 10z = -7$

multiply (5) by 13, gives:

$$13y + 130z = -91 \qquad (6)$$
$$13y + 18z = 21 \qquad (4)$$
$$112z = -112 \qquad \text{so that } z = -1$$
$$y + 10z = -7 \qquad (5)$$

thus $y - 10 = -7$,   or $y = -7 + 10$ so that $y = 3$

$$2x + 3y + 4z = 9 \quad (1)$$

therefore $2x + 9 - 4 = 9$ gives $2x = 4$ so that $x = 2$

CHECK on the given equation (3)

$$8 + 15 + 2 = 25$$

CHECK on the given equation (2)

$$6 - 6 + 3 = 3$$

CHECK on the given equation (1)

$$4 + 9 - 4 = 9.$$

There are further simple simultaneous equation exercises at the end of this chapter.

Linear equations

In the last example above, there were two variables $x + y$ and a question may require the calculation of the relationship between the two variables. The graph of a linear equation gives a straight line in the general form $y = a + bx$. The intercept of the line on the y-axis is a and the slope (gradient) of the line is variable b.

Some students, certainly those who came up the AAT route, will recall that this formula was used in forecasting techniques, as the "least-squares" method of regression analysis. Values of a and b were calculated from a time-series analysis.

Thus the graph of $y = 6x + 50$ would show:

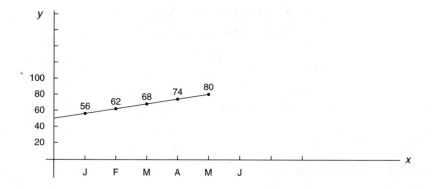

If, in this example, the y axis represents £'000 of sales and the x-axis, months of the year, we learn that, *on past performance*, the expected revenue increase is £6000 per month and the line can be projected (extrapolated), into the future.

A fuller example of the least-squares method is given below. We are given the output (x) and production cost (y) for five successive months. There are two tasks:

(i)   to calculate the output cost at 22,000 units and
(ii) to see if there is a close relationship between the output and the cost

Output X	Cost Y	XY	X^2	Y^2
20	82	1,640	400	6,724
16	70	1,120	256	4,900
24	90	2,160	576	8,100
22	85	1,870	484	7,225
18	73	1,314	324	5,329
$\sum X$ 100	$\sum Y$ 400	$\sum XY$ 8,104	$\sum X^2$ 2,040	$\sum Y^2$ 32,278

$\sum$ = Greek letter "sigma" meaning "the sum of"

n = Number of pairs of data = 5

$$b = \frac{(5 \times 8104) - (100 \times 400)}{(5 \times 2040) - 100^2}$$

$$= \frac{40,520 - 40,000}{10,200 - 10,000} = \frac{520}{200} = 2.6$$

$$a = \frac{400}{5} - 2.6 \times \frac{(100)}{5}$$
$$= 80 - (2.6 \times 20)$$
$$= 80 - 52 = 28$$

Therefore $Y = 28 + 2.6x$

The answers to the two tasks are:

(1) $28 + (2.6 \times 22) = £85,200$

(2) We calculate the *co-efficient of correlation* between x and y (see later in this chapter). As expected, the answer being almost 1, confirms a very close relationship between output and cost.

$$= \frac{520}{\sqrt{200 \times (5 \times 32,278 - 400^2)}}$$

$$= \frac{520}{\sqrt{200 \times 1390}}$$

$$= \frac{520}{527.3} = 0.98615$$

Quadratic equations

There are a type of non linear equation, in which one variable varies with the square of the other variable, and is expressed in the form:

$$y = ax^2 + bx + c$$

It is very unlikely that knowledge of quadratic equations will be required at managerial or subsequent levels

Before leaving the subject of algebra and equations, here are three examples showing how they may be of practical use in solving examination type questions. They are not scary at all!

Example 1

Mike and Mark have just finished a CIMA exam paper and they decide that it is time for refreshments. Mike orders two coffees and three buns, which in total cost £3.23. Mark orders three coffees and just one bun, totalling £2.92. We need to know the respective cost of a cup of coffee and a bun.

Let a cuppa be represented by "x" and a bun by "y"

Mike has $2x + 3y = 323$p
Mark has $3x + 1y = 292$p

Multiply Mark by 3 gives him $9x + 3y = 876$
Subtract Mike gives $-7x = -553$
So that x must be 79p

y therefore $= 292 - (3 \times 79)$ which equals $292 - 237 = 55$p

CHECK (on Mike's order) $(2 \times 79) + (3 \times 55) = 158 + 165 = 323$p $= £3.23$

Example 2

Sandra has a new product that she intends to sell direct to the public. She will experiment for two successive weeks at two different prices:

Week	Price (P)	Demand (D)
1	7	1050
2	9	950

Given that the relationship between price and demand is in the form, $P = xD + y$, what are the values of x and y?

Where $P = 7$, $D = 1050$ so $7 = 1050x + y$ (1)
Where $P = 9$, $D = 950$ so $9 = 950x + y$ (2)
Subtract $2 = -100x$
So that x must equal -0.02

Substitute into (1) $7 = -0.02 \times 1050 + y$
So that y must equal $7 + 21 = 28$

CHECK

$$x = -0.02 \quad \text{and} \quad y = 28$$
$$7 = -0.02(1050) + 28$$
$$7 = -21 + 28$$

If the Demand is 1000 units, the price will be:

$$P = -0.02(1000) + 28$$
$$P = -20 + 28$$
$$P = 8$$

Example 3

Phil buys 20 cases of Product A at £15.68 a case; 10 boxes of Product B at £16.40 per case; 12 pallets of Product C at £16.50 per pallet and a quantity of Product D, which cost £16.50 a case. In total, he spends £939.60. Each case of Product D contains 12 items. How many D items did he buy?

$$(20 \times 15.68) + (10 \times 16.40) + (12 \times 16.50) + (D \times 16.50) = 939.60$$
$$313.60 + 164.00 + 198.00 + (D \times 16.50) = 939.60$$
$$16.5D = 939.60 - 675.60 = 264.00$$
$$D = 264.00/16.5 = 16 \text{ cases}$$

Number of D items bought therefore is 192.

B   Accuracy and Approximation

The CIMA examiner may require you to express your answer to a calculation in a certain way, e.g. "to the nearest £'000". To refresh the knowledge of the main methods of "rounding", here are some self-test exercises, followed by the answers:

Questions

1   What is £625,496.27, to the nearest:
   (a) £1
   (b) £100
   (c) £1,000
   (d) £10,000
   (e) £100,000
   (f) £1,000,000
2   Express the sum of £15.27984, correct to:
   (a)   one decimal place
   (b)   two decimal places
   (c)   three decimal places

Solutions

1   (a) £625,496
   (b) £625,500
   (c) £625,000
   (d) £630,000
   (e) £600,000
   (f) £1,000,000
2   (a) 15.3
   (b) 15.28
   (c) 15.280

Remember two general rules of "rounding to the nearest":

  (i)   if your last number is between 0 and 4, round down and if it is between 5 and 9 round up. So that 16.1975 to the nearest three decimal places, is 16.198 and 27.0543, is 27.05
  (ii) Where you have a recurring number, cap it at the third decimal point figure. So that 127.666666, etc. would appear as $127.66\overline{6}$

C Analysing Data

This section will look at three areas which relate to the gathering and interpretation of data – Averages, Measures of Dispersion and Index Numbers. They have in common that they are measures which represent a group of data, or movements therein.

Averages

Let us start with an average measure that everybody knows something about – the arithmetic mean of ungrouped data, which is widely used and generally understood. It is depicted as x and is calculated by dividing the sum of the values of items by the number of items.

Values	17, 56, 34, 8, 19, 107, 53, 22
Sum of values	$316 \div 8$
X	$= 39.5$

In dealing with a *frequency distribution*, the arithmetic mean is found by multiplying each demand by its frequency, adding the resultant calculation and dividing by the number of frequencies. For daily pint deliveries by the milkman, we may have as follows:

A Demand	B Frequency	$A \times B$
1	22	22
2	15	30
3	10	30
4	4	16
5	6	30
	$\sum AB$	128

Here, $X = 128/57 = 2.24$ pints

To calculate the X of grouped data, we work on the assumed mid point of each group, multiplied by the frequency. In a bakery, the daily demand for cakes produced and sold may be:

Demand	A Frequency	B Demand mid-point	A × B
> 0 ≤ 10	88	5	440
> 10 ≤ 20	39	15	585
> 20 ≤ 30	22	25	550
> 30 ≤ 40	15	35	525
> 40 ≤ 50	11	45	495
> 50 ≤ 60	5	55	275
	$\sum A$ 180		$\sum AB$ 2870

X = 15.94 cakes

Finally, to calculate the *average of combined data*, we divide the sum of the values of items by the number of items. Thus, in one rugby team the average age is 22: in another, it is 25, this gives:

$$15 \times 22 = 330$$
$$15 \times 25 = 375$$

A sum of the values of $705 \div 30$ items $= 23.5$ years

Each of these measures may be criticised. In the first three calculations, it is impossible for the calculated average to be exactly true: it may be distorted by high or low values and in the grouped data calculation, it is assumed that the frequencies occur evenly over the class interval range. But they are all easy to calculate and can be widely understood to represent a set of data.

Having looked at the mean, we can move on to the median and the mode. The median is the value of the middle number of a group, once that group has been placed in an ascending order of magnitude:

Data given:

15, 9, 2, 17, 3, 22, 8, 10, 7, 6, 18   (11 numbers)

Ascending order:

2, 3, 6, 7, 8, 9, 10, 15, 17, 18, 22

The middle number is that in the sixth position $= 9$. If 9 was not in the original data, there would be ten numbers and the median would be $(8 + 10)/2 = 9$

ℇ is that value that occurs most frequently in a group:

en:

13, 19, 7, 41, 26, 18, 13, 15, 37, 40

Here, the mode is 13. If there were two 15's in the group as well, there would be two modes (bimodal) – 13 and 15.

As with the arithmetic average (mean), these values are easy to calculate, but the median fails to reflect the full range of values and needs tiresome re-ordering. The mode only reflects the most common value (there may be two or more) and ignores the remaining information which is available.

In looking at the mean, median and mode, we have considered three different "measures of central tendency". Each is a figure that can be said to be typical of the population that we are considering and in a particular circumstance, one may be more appropriate than another. A measure of central tendency is very useful if we wished, say, to compare ourselves with the rest of our competitor companies, or to compare two populations. What it does not do, is to tell us a great deal about the population from which it comes. We might like to know more about a population before we start to make fair comparisons and draw meaningful conclusions.

It could be that in making a business decision, the profits of two available options, both have a mean of £20,000. What you do not know is that option A has a profit range from (£5000) to £85,000 and that option B's range is much narrower at £17,000–£23,000. B has a much lower potential maximum, but no chance of going into the red!

How, therefore can we measure and compare the spread of data in a population? To do that we need to employ measures of dispersion.

Measures of Dispersion

While the arithmetic mean, or average, of a group of data is a useful representative of the whole, it gives no idea of the range or distribution (dispersion) of values in that group. To plug that gap, there are a number of statistical techniques which help us to understand more about the data being analysed.

Accepting that a median (Q2) is the value of the middle member of an array, the lower quartile (Q1) is the value below which 25% of the population falls, and at the other end is the upper quartile (Q3). Thus, if we had 11 items in our data, the quartiles would be:

$$Q1 = 11 \times \tfrac{1}{4} = 2.75 \qquad \text{(the 3rd item)}$$
$$Q3 = 11 \times \tfrac{3}{4} = 8.25 \qquad \text{(the 9th item)}$$
$$Q2 = 11 \times \tfrac{1}{2} = 5.5 \qquad \text{(the 6th item)}$$

Developing this further, the inter quartile range (IQR) is the difference between the Q1 and Q3 values and this shows the range of values in the middle half of the population. If the population has extreme values, the IQR is a useful measure of dispersion, but with no distorting extreme values, it is more useful to calculate either the mean deviation, or the standard deviation. The standard deviation in particular, is a very important measure of dispersion, as it takes into account the value of every observation in a population and its calculation and interpretation should be known for Managerial Level studies. As also should the *co-efficient of variation*, which compares the spread of the two variations. The mean deviation shows by how much, on average, each item in the distribution differs in value from the mean. Examples will now put this text into practice:

Calculation of mean deviation

Consider the number of overtime hours worked each month by 80 employees

More than	Not more than	Frequency (f)
0	10	5
10	20	8
20	30	18
30	40	20
40	50	25
50	60	4
		80

Mid-point (x)	f	fx	$lx - \bar{x}l$	$f(lx - \bar{x}l)$
5	5	25	28	140
15	8	120	18	144
25	18	450	8	144
35	20	700	2	40
45	25	1,125	12	300
55	4	220	22	88
Σf	80	Σfx 2,640		856

$lx - \overline{x}l$ is the difference between each value of x and the arithmetic mean (x) of the distribution

$$(\overline{x} = 2640/80 = 33)$$

The mean deviation is $8560/80 = 10.7$ hours

Calculation of the variance and the standard variation

The Variance (σ^2), is the average of the squared mean deviation for each value in a distribution. The standard deviation is the square root of the variance.

Both of these important measures, are, of course relegated to nasty formula (see Appendix D) But we will try the examples below without looking at the formulae.

Following on from the employee overtime example already used in calculating the mean deviation:

Mid-point	f	x	fx
5	5	25	125
15	8	225	1,800
25	18	625	11,250
35	20	1,225	24,500
45	25	2,025	50,625
55	4	3,025	12,100
	80		88,300

Arithmetic mean x $= 33$

Variance $= 88,300/80 - (33)^2$
$\qquad = 1103.75 - 1089 = 14.75$ hours

Standard deviation $= \sqrt{14.75} = 3.84$ hours

And finally.... The co-efficient of variation, compares the spreads of two distributions and, mercifully, involves a friendly formula:

$$\text{Standard deviation/mean}$$

The co-efficient of variation from our earlier example is $3.84/33 = 0.116$

Taking a further example and given the following two sets of data:

	A	B
Mean	150	160
Standard deviation	70	72
Coefficient of variation	0.583	0.450

B has a higher standard deviation and its relative spread is smaller than A.

Index numbers

As with the "average", there will be no Managerial Level candidates who have not heard of indexation and index numbers. An index is a figure derived from a system or scale and is representative of movements within that scale. Well-known UK national indices include the FTSE 100 and the monthly Retail Price Index (RPI). Index numbers when compared and plotted over time provide a standardised way of comparing values. They are extensively used in both public and private sectors of the economy and their use can pop up anywhere in the examination room.

An index is normally related to a base date or base year where its value is usually taken as 100. For example, the base for the RPI is January 1987. In February 2007, the RPI stood at 203.1, an increase of 103.1 points and (since the base was 100) an increase of a similar amount percent. The more recent Consumer Price Index (CPI) base is January 2005.

A simple, hypothetical, example related to movements in consumer prices in Ruritania over a period of years, shows:

20 X 1	120.3
20 X 2	122.8
20 X 3	126.4
20 X 4	138.7
20 X 5	149.3
20 X 6	150.1
20 X 7	151.6
20 X 8	151.3

Over the period covered, the Index rise is 31 points or an increase of 25.8%. It shows a significant increase in the middle years, with price inflation well under control (and even reducing) at the end. Between 20×4 and 20×6, there was a rise of 11.4 points or 8.2%.

This method of calculation is termed, for obvious reasons, the *fixed base* method. A *chain base* method shows the rate of change from year to year. In the example the rate of change between 20×2 and 20×3 is 3.6 points (2.9%) and from 20 X 3 to 20 X 4 is 12.3 points (9.7%)

Indices may also cover more than one item (the RPI covers over 10,000 prices of a wide range of commodities), when it is termed a composite index and as with the RPI, weightings may be used to reflect the relative importance of items within the index.

One of the more practical uses of indexation, is in the performance evaluation (or value for money) aspects of the work of the management accountant. In comparing two related sets of figures, indexation may be used to ensure that like is compared with like.

A well-known example of this, is to compare the amount of money spent on advertising a product, with the volume of sales over a similar period:

	20 X 1	20 X 2	20 X 3	20 X 4	20 X 5	20 X 6
Advertising (20 X 3 = 100)	94	98	100	120	129	137
Sales (20 X 1 = 100)	225	265	287	288	307	322

Here, the index for sales was set several years before that for advertising expenditure. If the sales figures are rebased to 20 X 3, the indices for sales become:

Sales	78	92	100	107	106	112

which puts a different slant on what is happening and shows that sales are lagging behind advertising expenditure. (A quicker way to arrive at this conclusion is to calculate the % movement, between the first and the last year, which give Advertising up 46% and Sales up 44%!.)

A final comment on indices concerns the word "real", beloved of politicians. The Chancellor of the Exchequer may announce "that NHS spending next year is to rise by 7%". If general inflation is increasing at 4%, that gives a 3% increase "in real terms", i.e. 3% of "new money".

D Probability, Payoff, Forecasting and Correlatic

The arithmetical and statistical techniques so far mentioned in this chapter are valuable in themselves and can be very useful in dealing with questions in any CIMA Professional Examination Paper.

Even more important, are those areas now to be considered, which are likely to form whole questions, or the major part of questions, in your examinations.

Probability and expected values

Measuring the likelihood of something happening, or the extent to which it will probably happen, probabilities (P), are traditionally expressed as a proportion, a percentage, a ratio, or a number from 1 (a certainty) to 0 (an impossibility). In any given scenario, the probabilities involved will always sum to 1 or (100%).

A basic rule of assessing probability, is to divide the number of ways of achieving a desired result by the total number of possible outcomes. Thus, a coin tossed will either come down heads or tails (but not in Estonia!). In either event, the solution following the basic rule is $\frac{1}{2}$, expressed as 50% or 0.500.

Similarly, the probability of a red card being drawn from a pack of playing cards is 26/52, also 0.500; of a spade being drawn $13/52 = \frac{1}{4} = 0.250$; of an ace being drawn is $4/52 = 1/13 = 0.077$ and of a black ace being drawn, after a non-Court card has already been selected is 2/51 or 0.039. Finally, the probability of getting an ace or a spade from the pack is:

(Ace) $4/52 + $ (Spade) $13/52 - 1/52^* = 16/52 = 4/13 = 0.307 (30.7\%)$

* the ace might be the ace of spades

Question
As an example, what is the probability (P), that a card taken at random from a pack of 52, is either a picture card (J, Q, K) or the 7, 8, 9 of clubs?

Solution
Call picture card event A: call club card event B

These events are mutually exclusive (they can't both happen)

$$P \text{ of A is } \frac{12}{52} = \frac{3}{13} \quad \text{(or 0.230 or 23\%)}$$
$$P \text{ of B is } \frac{3}{52} \quad \text{(or 0.057 or 5.7\%)}$$

So that the P of either A or B is:

$$\frac{12}{52} + \frac{3}{52} = \frac{15}{52}$$

(or 0.288 or 28.8%)

Question

A box of biscuits contains five chocolate biscuits (C) and one lemon biscuit (L). Eleanor takes out three biscuits at random, one at a time and eats them. Find the probability (P) that:

    (a)   she eats three chocolate biscuits
    (b)   the last biscuit is chocolate

Solution

We can relegate this problem to a 'probability tree' diagram and work in fractions as follows:

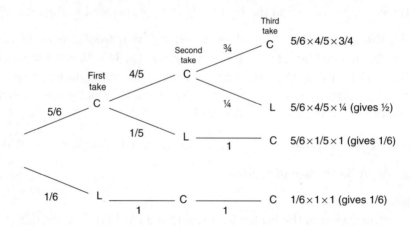

    (a)   3C are shown only by the top path:

$$5/6 \times 4/5 \times {}^{3}/_{4} = 60/120 = {}^{1}/_{2} \text{ or } 50\%$$

    (b)   the third biscuit having a C is shown by the other paths:

$$^{1}/_{2} + 1/6 + 1/6 = 5/6$$

NB: A quicker way to do this, since there is only one outcome where the C is not pulled last is as follows:

$$P = \frac{5}{6} \times \frac{4}{5} \times \frac{1}{4} = \frac{20}{120} = \frac{1}{6}$$

So the P that the third biscuit is as follows:

C must be $1 - 1/6 = 5/6$

As well as calculating probabilities, the CIMA student will also meet the concept of *Expected Values (EVs)* defined in the *Official Terminology* as "the financial forecast of the outcome of a course of action, multiplied by the probability of achieving that outcome".

In calculating what is the expected daily output for a 5-day period, the following probabilities are assessed, on the basis of past performance:

Day	Units produced	×	Probability	=	Expected Value
1	4,500		0.200		900
2	5,750		0.350		2,010
3	6,000		0.150		900
4	5,250		0.200		1,050
5	4,500		0.100		450
			1.000		5,310

A rather extreme position, but it does show the principle involved! For planning purposes, the figure of 5310 units being produced in that week would be used since past experience tells us that this is what will probably happen – i.e. is expected.

EVs may also be used in investment decisions, where the general rule is that a project with a positive EV should be accepted and one with a negative EV should not be proceeded with. In management accounting decisions involving both reviews and costs, EVs may be employed, as in the next example, to calculate an expected profit.

Example 4

A company has three mutually exclusive investment options, with the following expected returns and probabilities. The task is to decide which option should be chosen.

Option 1		Option 2		Option 3	
Return (£'000)	P	Return (£'000)	P	Return (£'000)	P
60,000	0.75	67,000	0.6	(9,000)	0.1
90,000	0.25	60,000	0.3	90,000	0.1
		20,000	0.1	88,000	0.8

The EV for each option is as follows:

$$£$$

1	$45,000 + 22,500$	$= 67,500$
2	$40,200 + 18,000 + 2000 = 60,200$
3	$(900) + 900 + 70,400$	$= 70,400$

The balance of probabilities is that Option 3 would offer the best deal, but there is an outside chance it will make a loss. Both 1 and 2 have lower returns, but they are not significantly lower. In addition, Options 1 and 2 show positive returns under all circumstances.

The CIMA *Official Terminology* definition of EVs given earlier, is in fact the definition of EV/Payoff. Both terms are concerned with what an organisation expects to gain from a certain course of action. That payoff will depend on a number of circumstances which are unknown when the decision to proceed is taken.

A Payoff Table is simply a matrix to show the potential consequences of circumstances/action taken and an example is now shown.

A shopkeeper has to decide how many dozen perishable cream gateaux to purchase every day. Experience has shown that the demand possibilities are

Demand	P
1	0.2
2	0.4
3	0.4

Each gateau costs £15 and sells for £30. Any unsold items are thrown away. Using EVs, how many should be bought daily?

Demand	Daily order		
	1	**2**	**3**
1	£15	0	(£15)
2	£15	£30	£15
3	£15	£30	£45

For each eventuality sale revenue is matched against cost. Using the P given, the EV daily profit is:

EV Order 1	£15	$= £15$
EV Order 2	$(0.2 \times 0) + (0.4 \times 30) + (0.4 \times 30)$	$= £24$
EV Order 3	$(0.2 \times -15) + (0.4 \times 15) + (0.4 \times 45)$	$= £21$

Therefore, to maximise profit, two dozen gateaux should be ordered daily.

You will meet such calculations in your Managerial Level studies under the name "maximax, maximin".

Forecasting techniques

Another important examination area, especially in the P1 Paper, with its syllabus references to budgeting, is the technique of forecasting based on past data as a guide to the future. Here will look at two aspects of forecasting – time-series analysis and correlation/regression.

Time-series analysis

A time series is a set of data recorded over time. If plotted on a graph, the data forms a historigram. The formula employed in time-series analysis may be expressed as:

$$Y = T + S + C + I$$

Which represent the four components of a time series and may be translated as follows:

Actual = trend + seasonal variations + cyclical variations
+ irregular (random) variations

This is the assessment formula for the *additive* model: later in the text, we will meet the *multiplicative* or *proportional* model, in which the formula is $Y = T \times S \times I$ (as in the Appendix C example).

The trend may be defined as the basic underlying movement in the actual data. Cyclical variations take place over long time periods. Seasonal variations are those which form a regular, short term, pattern (e.g. beer sales are higher in the summer). By their very nature, Random variations cannot be forecast with any degree of accuracy and, along with cyclical variations are not met in the CIMA examination calculations. In practical terms, therefore, we are left with $Y = T + S$ (additive model) or $Y = T \times S$ (multiplicative model).

Before using past data to forecast what might happen in the future, we firstly need to identify the trend and any seasonal variations around that trend. The underlying movement of a historigram, may be found by drawing a "line of best fit" through the plotted data. Because this relies on the human eye, it is a pretty inaccurate method and can effectively be discarded, after noting that it exists.

In considering linear equations earlier in this chapter, we met, secondly, the "least-squares" method of regression analysis. An example there, showed the basis of calculating a straight line trend underlying a set of past date.

The third method of finding the trend, is that which employs moving averages to both establish the trend and isolate the seasonal variations, by a process of averaging. To exemplify how all this works, we will take the following output (in thousands), of factory units produced over a 3-week period:

| | | Units produced | |
Day	Week 1	Week 2	Week 3
Monday	150	160	170
Tuesday	210	200	210
Wednesday	160	180	190
Thursday	250	280	280
Friday	100	90	80

The sequential steps, having rearranged all the data vertically are firstly to calculate a moving average of each weeks output. Here, we will average in consecutive blocks of 5: this could be in "threes", or "sevens", depending on how much data we are dealing with.

Secondly, each 5-day moving average is divided by 5 to give the trend (T) and in the end column the seasonal variation (S) is obtained by comparing each trend with its relevant actual output (Y).

Thus, on Wednesday of Week 2, $Y = T + S$ translates as $180 = 182 + -2$:

Week 1	Output (Y)	5-day average	Trend (T)	Seasonal variation (S)
Monday	150			
Tuesday	210			
Wednesday	160	870*	174**	−14
Thursday	250	880	176	+74
Friday	100	870	174	−74
Week 2				
Monday	160	890	178	−18
Tuesday	200	920	184	+16
Wednesday	180	910	182	−2
Thursday	280	920	184	+96
Friday	90	930	186	−96
Week 3				
Monday	170	940	188	−18
Tuesday	210	940	188	+22
Wednesday	190	930	186	+4
Thursday	280			
Friday	80			

* $(150 + 210 + 160 + 250 + 100)$
** $870 \div 5$

From this, a clear picture is emerging. Good production days are Tuesday and Thursday, Wednesday is mixed and the days either side of the weekend are poor. Over the period, the Trend has risen from 174 to 186, but has not done so in a consistent pattern.

The next step is to average and then cancel out the seasonal variations around the trend, so that the seasonal variations sum to zero

	M	T	W	TH	F		Totals
Week 1			−14	+74	−74		
Week 2	−18	+16	−2	+96	+96		
Week 3	−18	+22	+4				
	−36	+38	−12	+170	−170	=	+104
Average	−18	+19	−6	+85	−85	=	−109
							−5

The end column totals show an excess of −5, so we must add +1 to each daily average, to get this end total to zero.

M	T	W	TH	F		Totals
−17	+20	−5	+86	−84	=	+106
						−106

To use this information in forecasting, the trend line must firstly be extrapolated, but how can this be done, if it is not moving in a straight line? The answer is to calculate the average daily movement of the Trend line.

Week 1	Wednesday	174
Week 3	Wednesday	186
	Over 10 movements	+12
Average increase per movement (day)		+1.2

We can therefore extrapolate the line forward at +1.2 each day. On Friday of Week 3, it will stand at $186 + (2 \times 1.2) = 188.4$.

On this principle, the trend line will be at 193.2 on Thursday of Week 4 and since the average seasonal variation on a Thursday, is +86, the forecast output for that day will be 279,200 units.

We saw earlier that this method of calculating the seasonal variation is called the additive model, where variations are expressed as + or − from the trend. The Multiplicative or Proportional model works on exactly the same principle, but the seasonal variation is expressed as a percentage of the Trend and average variations are summed to 500 in this case, as there are 5 days involved. A full week, would sum to 700.

Having done all that, what credence would you give to forecasts prepared on either model? An almost universal answer would be "not a lot", being based on

what is history and taking no account of the many potential current and fu.
developments. Don't worry – just know how to do each method and rememb
that examiners love it!

Correlation

Forecasting calculations, like the examples looked at in this chapter, have been
based on two variables, e.g. time and output: advertising expenditure and sales
revenues. Correlation considers the measurement between these two related
variables. Measures of correlation are expressed as r and fall between +1
(perfect "good" correlation) and −1 (perfect "not good" correlation). The nearer
r is to either +1 or −1, the stronger the relationship between the variables.

The correlation co-efficient, r, is calculated by a frightening looking formula
which you will find in Appendix D at the end of this book. We will here, try a
calculation without looking at the formula as we did with the "least-squares"
exercise in Section A of this chapter.

Example 5

Given, for six consecutive months are factory output (thousands of units) and
the cost (in £thousands) of that output. The task is to calculate the correlation
between the two variables X and Y.

Month	X Output	Y Cost
5	4	18
6	6	22
7	3	15
8	8	26
9	7	24
10	10	29

Firstly, put these details into the following template:

	X	Y	XY	X^2	Y^2
	4	18	72	16	324
	6	22	132	36	484
	3	15	45	9	225
	8	26	208	64	676
	7	24	168	49	576
	10	29	290	100	841
$\sum$	38	134	915	274	3,126

$(\sum X^2 = 1444 : \sum Y^2 = 17,956)$

149

There are 6 months involved in the application of the frightening formula:

$$= \frac{(6 \times 915) - (38 \times 134)}{\sqrt{(6 \times 274 - 1444) \times (6 \times 3126 - 17{,}956)}}$$

$$= \frac{5490 - 5092}{\sqrt{200 \times 800}}$$

$$= \frac{398}{400} = 0.995$$

There is thus almost perfect positive correlation between output and costs, as might be expected, given the scenario.

E   Compounding and Discounting

This, the final section of Chapter 4, considers two very important subjects which are great examination favourites. Compounding, the result of investing money over time and its opposite, discounting (bringing future cash flows back to present values), may pop up throughout the professional level studies. As there are very many types of calculations only the main, more usual, ones will be considered here. You will, no doubt, meet others in your studies.

Simple interest and annual percentage rate

Before looking at compounding proper, let us clear calculations involving simple interest. £1000 invested at 5% for 3 years will yield £50 annually and £150 over the period of the investment. If it is invested for 90 days, the gross return will be £1000 × 5% × (90/365) = £12.33 gross. A further variation on this simple interest theme is the annual percentage rate (APR), where the rate of interest actually charged on a debt, is higher than its nominal (or face) value.

If interest on a debt of £1000 is 10% p.a. and £400 is to be repaid 6 months into the year, the rate of interest actually paid is:

£1000 for 6 months	500
£600 for 6 months	300
	£800

In reality, the interest due to be paid (£100) is on an effective debt of £800 giving an annual percentage rate of 12.5%.

Compounding

With simple interest investments, the money earned is taken out at the end of each year. Thus, each year begins with the sum of the original investment. With compound interest, the return is added to the original investment and then earns interest on interest. Following the earlier simple interest example, our £1000 investment will grow to £1157.625 over 3 years:

$$\text{Final Value } (V) = \text{Investment} \times (1+r)$$
$$V = 1000 \times (1.05)^3$$
$$V = 1000 \times 1.1576$$
$$V = £1157.625$$

thereby gaining an extra £7.625 gross interest.

As is often the case, the interest rate may change during the period of the investment. For example, a sum of £20,000 is invested for 6 years – 2 years @ 6%: 1 year @ 5% and the final three years at 5.5%. This would yield:

$$= £20,000 \times (1.06)^2 \times (1.05) \times (1.055)^3$$
$$= 20,000 \times (1.1236 \times 1.05 \times 1.174)$$
$$= £27,701.23$$

A typical examination question may require the calculation of the amount to be periodically set aside (into a sinking fund) to settle a liability or replace an asset, sometime in the future. The sum to be calculated is that, which suitably invested will grow (accrue) to the required sum at the relevant time.

Example 6

A company wishes to replace a new machine in 5 years time, when a cost of £100,000 is envisaged. With interest @ 12%, what amount (A) should be set aside, in equal annual amounts starting now?

$$100,000 = \frac{A(1.12^5 - 1)}{1.12 - 1}$$

$$100,000 = \frac{A(0.7623)}{0.12}$$

$$100,000 = A(6.3525)$$

$$A = \frac{100,000}{6.3525}$$

$$A = £15,471.83$$

Discounting

This is the opposite of compounding and is based on the principle that if we need to have a certain amount of money available at a given future time, how much needs to be invested now.

Example 7

We need £21,000 to be available in 3 years time and can invest at 7%. The amount to be invested now (x) is:

$$21,000 = x(1.07)^3$$
$$21,000 = x \times 1.225$$
$$x = \frac{21,000}{1.225}$$
$$x = £17,143$$

This tells us that with inflation at 7%, £21,000 in 3 years time is the equivalent of £17,143 today (i.e. at present values).

The use of discounting that students will be most likely to meet in examinations, is in net present value (NPV) calculations. NPV is defined by CIMA as "the difference between the sum of the projected discounted cash inflows and outflows attributable to a capital investment or other long term project".

NPV calculations are typically used to make investment decisions where there is a choice of action. The technique brings all future cash flows back to today's (present) values so that like is compared with like in decision making as shown in Example 8.

Example 8

A hospital has the choice between two new laundry machines. Machine 1 costs £100,000 now and has a 5-year life. It will make reductions in present annual expenditure in each of the next 5 years of £15,000, £30,000, £50,000, £37,000 and £12,000.

Machine 2 costs £150,000 now, has a 7-year life and brings annual benefits over that period of £22,000, £36,000, £36,000, £45,000, £33,000, £21,000 and £6000. There is a £12,000 major overhaul in year 3.

The cost of capital in each case is 10%

Each set of figures is placed in the following template:

Year	Cash flow	×	Discount factor	=	Present value

The initial outlay is always shown as year 0 and the initial benefit is assumed to accrue in 12 months time – year 1. Cash outflows are shown in brackets.

The discount factors can be looked up in NPV tables (as in Appendix D), or in the absence of these, you may calculate your own, as follows (at 10%):

Year 1 $1/1.10 = 0.9090$
Year 2 $1/(1.10)2 = 0.8264$
Year 3 $1/(1.10)3 = 0.751$, etc.

Our NPV calculations for the two machine choices can now be done:

Machine 1

Year	Flow	×	discount factor	=	Present value
0	(100,000)		1.000		(100,000)
1	15,000		0.909		13,635
2	30,000		0.826		24,780
3	50,000		0.751		37,550
4	37,000		0.683		25,271
5	12,000		0.621		7,452
				NPV =	£8,688

Machine 2

Year	Flow	×	discount factor	=	Present value
0	(150,000)		1.000		(150,000)
1	22,000		0.909		19,998
2	36,000		0.826		29,736
3	36,000		0.751		27,036
	(12,000)		0.683		(8,196)
4	15,000		0.683		30,735
5	33,000		0.621		20,493
6	21,000		0.564		11,844
7	6,000		0.513		3,078
				NPV =	£(15,276)

Since machine 1 has a positive NPV, it should be the choice purchase on financial grounds. There may, however be other factors (ease of operation and maintenance and eventual replacement) that might cause machine 2 to be selected.

If both options had a negative NPV but it was essential to have one of the machines, then the option with the smaller negative NPV would be chosen.

Internal rate of return

An alternative to the NPV method of investment evaluation is the internal rate of return (IRR). This is the discount rate (or cost of capital) which gives a NPV of zero (when the present values of costs and benefits are equal). The IRR method is used to indicate if a project is viable if it exceeds the company's minimum acceptable rate of return. Thus if a company expects to return 10% on new capital expenditure, a project which gives an IRR above, 10% would be viable.

Example 9: IRR calculation

A new production facility costing £80,000 now, is expected to generate additional revenues over a 3-year period of £46,000, £28,000 and £16,000 respectively. We need to calculate the IRR, as the company will only invest if the return is greater than $7\frac{1}{2}$%.

Firstly, we will calculate roughly what the IRR will be:

$$\text{Take} \quad \frac{2}{3}\frac{(\text{Profit})}{(\text{Cost})}\%$$

$$= \frac{2}{3}\frac{(10,000)}{(80,000)}\%$$

$$= \frac{20,000}{240,000}\% = 0.083 = 8.3\%$$

so that our IRR is in the region of 8%

Using our earlier NPV template, this gives a NPV of £(704). Since this is a negative, the IRR must be less then 8%.

The net present value (using that template) at 7% gives a positive figure of £510. The IRR therefore lies somewhere between 7% and 8% and can be found in the following way:

$$7\% + \left[\frac{510}{(510+704)} \times 8 - 7\% \right]\%$$

$$= 7\% + [0.42]\%$$

$$= 7.42\%$$

and since this return is less than that of 7.5% in the company's investment policy, it will not be proceeded with.

Annuities

Finally, in this chapter on business mathematics, we will look at an annuity, defined by CIMA as "a fixed periodic payment which continues either for a specified time, or until the occurrence of a specific event".

Managerial Level students who sat the CBA Paper on *Business Mathematics*, will have met a syllabus requirement to be able to calculate the present value of an annuity, but other students may not have come across them in earlier studies.

Example 10

I have £50,000 to invest today @ 6%, to begin receiving a 10-year annuity in a year's time – What annual amount will I then receive?

$$A = \frac{50{,}000}{\left[\frac{1}{0.06}\left(1 - \frac{1}{(1.06)^{10}}\right)\right]}$$

$$A = \frac{50{,}000}{\left[16.667\left(1 - \frac{1}{1.790}\right)\right]}$$

$$A = \frac{50{,}000}{[16.667\,(1 - 0.558)]}$$

$$A = \frac{50{,}000}{(16.667 \times 0.442)}$$

$$A = \frac{50{,}000}{7.3668} \quad £6787.2$$

Rather than go through all this calculation, just like NPVs, we can calculate the annuity factor by consulting Cumulative Present Value Tables. These show, for a 10-year period @ 6%, a factor of 7.360, as against the 7.3668 above (due to rounding). The annual receipt, using this slightly lower figure is £6793.48.

Revision Questions

1   A shopkeeper buys an item for £10 and sells it for £50, but if it is not sold by the end of the day, it will be thrown away. The likely demand is given as follows:

Demand	Probability
0	0.3
1	0.4
2	0.3

Requirement

Advise the shopkeeper on how many he should stock each day.

2   Hans Siegfried is preparing to plan his production budget solely on the basis of past performance. His business works on a quarterly reporting system and units of umbrellas and parasols produced, for the past 3 years are given below:

	Units produced		
Quarter	2003	2004	2005
Spring	5020	5000	4900
Summer	4450	5100	5200
Autumn	4000	4100	3900
Winter	2790	2780	2500

Requirements
   (a)   calculate the trend and seasonal variations on the multiplicative model;
   (b)   calculate the likely production of units in the spring of 2007;
   (c)   give six reasons why budgeting on this basis is not recommended.

3   "Things are going pretty well!" Hans Siegfried proudly tells you one afternoon. " In fact, I am thinking of buying a new spoke making machine, to assist in the manufacture of my quality products" You find out that he is considering two options:

Machine A will cost £55,000, has a life of 5 years and will save energy costs in year 1 of £8000, increasing by 2% in each of the next 4 years.

Machine B currently costs £80,000 and will last for 8 years. It will save £9000 in each of years 1–6 and £7000 in years 7 and 8. In year 4, it will need a £1500 overhaul.

Hans is proposing to borrow the money at 9% and he is insistent that he will buy one of them, of which there are only two worldwide suppliers.

Requirements
Advise Hans on the basis of NPV calculations

  (a) which machine would be preferable on financial grounds.
  (b) what other non financial factors should be considered before making a decision.

4   At 9%, the NPV of a proposal is (£15.9 m), but at 7%, the NPV shows a positive £14.4 m

Requirements
Calculate the IRR (a) by the formula method and (b) by interpolation.

5   An annuity pays £13,000 at the end of each year, until the death of the purchaser. At an interest rate of 6%, what is the present value of the annuity if the purchaser lives for (a) 10 years and (b) 20 years after purchase?

Requirements
Calculate the two present values indicated, using annuity tables for (a) and the formula in (b).

Solutions to Revision Questions

1   This is a question that can be solved using the production of a Payoff Table (in £per day) and the subsequent calculation of EVs.

Payoff Table		Probability		Order	
			0	1	2
Demand	0	0.3	0	−10	−20
	1	0.4	0	40	30
	2	0.3	0	40	80

Expected Values

If the daily order is 0, then the payoff is £0

If the daily order is 1, the payoff is $(-10 \times 0.3) + (40 \times 0.4) + (40 \times 0.3) = 25$

If the daily order is two, the payoff is, on the same basis, 30.

The optimal order, on the basis of the EV calculation, is two items daily. There is a risk of a loss of £20 a day, compared with an order of 1. Over time, however, a daily order of 2 should give an expected daily profit of £5.

2	Year/ Season		Units	Fourquarter Total (Moving)	Average (÷4)	Trend- Midpoint of Two	Seasonal Variation (% rounded)
	2003	S	5,020				
		S	4,450				
				16,260	4,065		
		A	4,000			4,062.5	98*
				16,240	4,060		
		W	2,790			4,141.25	67
				16,890	4,222.5		
	2004	S	5,000			4,235	119
				16,990	4,247.5		
		S	5,100			4,246.25	120
				16,980	4,245		
		A	4,100			4,232.5	97
				16,880	4,220		
		W	2,780			4,232.5	66
				16,980	4,245		

Year/ Season		Units	Fourquarter Total (Moving)	Average (÷4)	Trend- Midpoint of Two	Seasonal Variation (% rounded)
2005	S	4,900			4,220	116
			16,780	4,195		
	S	5,200			4,160	125
			16,500	4,125		
	A	3,900				
	W	2,500				

* 4,000 ÷ 4062.5

Year	Season S	S	A	W	Total
2003			98	67	
2004	119	120	97	66	
2005	116	125			
Total	235	245	195	133	
Average	117.5	122.5	97.5	66.5	404
Residual	−1.0	−1.0	−1.0	−1.0	−4
	116.5	121.5	96.5	65.5	400

Having done all that, we can then round the seasonal variations to:

Spring   116
Summer   121
Autumn   97
Winter   66   making sure that the total comes to 400.

(b)   Over this period, the trend has moved from 4062.5 to 4160, an increase of 97.5 in 7 quarters. This gives an increase of (say) 14 per quarter. The last trend reading is 4160 in the summer of 2005. By the Spring of 2007, there will be another six quarters, thus putting the trend line at $4160 + (6 \times 14) = 4244$. As the seasonal variation in the Spring is 116%, this suggests a likely production of 4923

(c)   The forecast relies solely upon what has happened in the past. In addition, it does not take into account fashion trends, the availability of materials, local and regional competition, cheap imports and (especially?) climate change. It also ignores any plans which Hans may have for the development/specialisation of his business.

3

Machine B

Year	Cashflow (£)	Factor	PV	
0	(80,000)	1.000	(80,000)	
1	9,000	0.917	8,253	
2	9,000	0.842	7,578	
3	9,000	0.772	6,948	
4	9,000	0.708	6,372	
4	(1,500)	0.708	(1,062)	
5	9,000	0.650	5,850	
6	9,000	0.596	5,364	
7	7,000	0.547	3,829	
8	7,000	0.502	3,514	NPV = (£33,354)

Machine A

Year	Cashflow	Factor	PV	
0	(55,000)	1.000	(55,000)	
1	8,000	0.917	7,336	
2	8,160	0.842	6,870	
3	8,223	0.772	6,425	
4	8,490	0.708	6,010	
5	8,660	0.650	5,629	NPV = (£22,730)

Poor Hans and after all that lovely forecasting! As he seems to be intent on buying one of these only options available, he will have to go for machine A, as having the lower negative NPV. On financial grounds, this is potentially very damaging to his business. It could be, however, that he knows something that we don't! Perhaps, he is getting in first, before his competition realizes that there are revolutionary new processes, with massive cost benefits?

Apart from the purely financial side, there are only two suppliers in the world. One (machine B) is 150 miles away in Nuremburg and the other is in New Zealand. He needs to consider the availability of servicing and spare parts; the potential disposal value and especially, what will replace them at the end of their working lives.

4   (a)

$$7\% + \left(\frac{14.4}{14.4 + 15.9} \times (9 - 7) \right) \%$$

$$= 7\% + \left(\frac{14.4}{30.3} \times 2 \right) \%$$

$$= 7\% + 0.95$$

$$= 7.95\%$$

(b)   There is a reasonable "balance" between a NPV of (15.9) and one of 14.4, suggesting that the IRR will be round about the middle of 7% and 9%, i.e. 8%. A graph may now be drawn, as follows, to broadly confirm a figure of just under 8%.

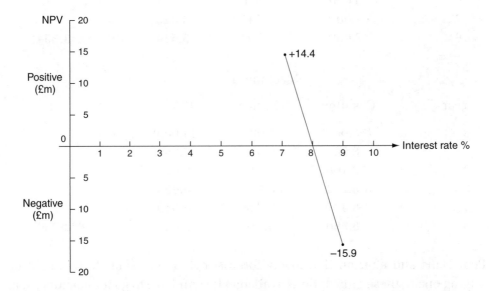

5   (a) If $n = 10$ and with an interest rate of 6%, the factor from cumulative present value Tables, is 7.360. The PV is, therefore £13,000 × 7.360 = £95,680

(b) With $n = 20$, the formulae method gives:

$$PV = 13,000 \times \left(\frac{1}{0.6} - \frac{1}{0.06^{20}} \right)$$

$$PV = 13,000 \times 11.4699 = £149,097$$

5

Budgeting Techniques

Put money in thy purse

(William Shakespeare)

Introduction

In the CIMA Managerial Level syllabus, budgeting and the principles of management accounting are linked together in Paper P1. This is fair enough, as there are many aspects of management accounting that are common areas. As an example, the principle of planning ahead, comparing actual results with the plan, investigating significant differences and taking corrective action are important stages in both standard costing and managing a sales or overheads budget.

Despite that, budgeting is being treated as a separate matter in this book since it has enough important material of its own to justify a separate chapter.

Budgeting forms the largest single element (30%) of Paper P1. If the analogy above with standard costing is taken into account, this iterative process of plan, control and adjust takes up 55% of the P1 syllabus. Paper P4 contains a syllabus reference to the content of a forward plan for the development and management of human resources. There are no express or implied references to budgeting in the two financial accounting Papers P7 and P8, other than cash flow forecasting in P7. This subject, however, will be met and is well covered in available texts on Paper P1. Paper P7 is more concerned with the using of cash forecasting in wider aspects of Treasury Management.

And what about the CBA syllabus? For those who did not study this syllabus, it is worth mentioning what was included in Paper CO1. That syllabus aims to test a student's ability to:

Explain and apply concepts and processes to determine product and service costs;

Explain direct, marginal and absorption costs and their use in pricing;

Apply CVP analysis and interpret the results;

Apply a range of costing and accounting systems;

Explain the role of budgets and standard costing within organisations;

Prepare and interpret budgets, standard costs and variance statements.

This syllabus content, reflects the fact that budgeting is a key element in the planning and control of a business. The principles of initially preparing the related ingredients of a master budget and its important relative, the cash budget, are required to be known. At this level, the student will have learnt that a Budget *preparation* is only half the story. The other half, *monitoring* is essential in spotting why the financial plan is not going as expected and taking corrective action to bring it back on course. Flexed, or flexible, budgets are also introduced but more of this later in the chapter.

Your Earlier Studies?

It is reasonable to expect that Managerial Level students will have met all of these preparation and control aspects of Budgeting, in whatever method of earlier studying brought them to this stage. AAT for example, in its Unit 9 (Contributing to the Planning and Control of Resources), requires competence in preparing forecasts of income and expenditure, drafting budget proposals and the monitoring of performance against budgets.

It is also pertinent to suggest that all students will have met budgeting principles in a more practical way, since many aspects of one's daily (monthly), life depend upon the forecasting of receipts and payments and the taking of early action to deal with cash shortages (credit card, bank overdraft) or surpluses (put a little more on deposit). There is thus a more personal regular involvement with cash, than with, say, process costing!

Budgeting Basics

The word budget comes from the French bougette; a diminutive of bouge, meaning a leather bag. Presumably, at one stage in the dim and distant that bag or purse, might have contained specie (coins of the realm). You will, no doubt, work out your own short and snappy definition. Perhaps it might relate to a "costed financial plan for a specific period". Where there is a doubt, or choice, about a definition, then turn to the excellent CIMA *Official Terminology* where you will find:

> The CIMA *Official Terminology* states that the Master Budget "consolidates all subsidiary budgets and is normally comprised of the budgeted profit and loss account, balance sheet and cash flow statement"

The P1 syllabus is substantially concerned with the preparation of a costed plan for a 12-month period. The "Annual Budget" "Master Budget" or just the "Budget" it might also be termed. What is important is that, regardless of terminology, you should envisage not one, but several related statements. The Master Budget will be the most often used term in P1 texts, so let us concentrate on exactly what that involves.

Planning for the future is a key responsibility of any business that wishes to succeed in an ever changing and fast moving environment. The ways in which these changes are reflected and how they impact on the work of the management accountant are dealt with in the final paragraphs of Chapter 1.

However, it is depicted in your chosen study text, you should appreciate that the annual budget fits in to a corporate planning framework. A well-known example of such a figure is *Anthony's hierarchy*, which reflects the following sequential stages in corporate planning:

Objectives	–	what do we want to achieve?
Strategy	–	how may we achieve our objectives?
Tactics	–	which chosen option(s) should we now employ?
Operations	–	what resources are required to do this?
Control	–	is our costed plan going according to plan?

Anthony presented this in the form of the following diagram:

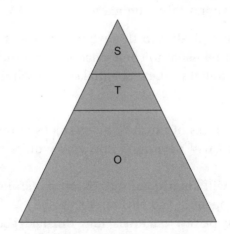

S	Strategic	– a Medium Term (3–5 years) to achieve your objectives (over-seen by the Directors and Chief Executive)
T	Tactical	– since these objectives must be achieved in stages (annual) what are we to do in the next year to help achieve that strategy (overseen by the Chief Executive with Departmental Heads)
O	Operational	– the rest of the employees meeting their bit of the annual tactical Plan in their day to day duties

You will see from this brief description, that the annual or Master Budget relates to T in achieving the Strategic Objectives of the business. These costed choices are approved as the Master Budget, which those at the day to day operational level are charged with responsibility for meeting. If all individual bits (responsibilities) are achieved with regular monitoring then collectively, the Master Budget is delivered and the Strategy is on course. By that time of course, the Business Directors will have reviewed the Strategy which will decide the "shape" of the next years courses of action (Tactics) and round we go again!

A   The Master and Subsidiary Budgets

There will be plenty of opportunity in your studies to get to know these related statements pretty well. The purpose of the Master Budget is to bring the subsidiary budgets together into a summary forecast of income and expenditure for the ensuing financial period – usually 12 months. The Subsidiary Budgets contain the detail to support this summary.

There is a sequential logicality to this whole process, but you have to start somewhere. It would be usual to commence with a prudent forecast of sales units and revenues. From this, the sequential steps, each requiring a Subsidiary Budget are:

- Decide the quantities of finished goods stocks at the beginning and end of the year (this will determine how many units you actually need to *manufacture*).
- From this, you will know quantities of *raw materials* to order, again after adjustment for opening and closing stocks.
- The conversion of raw materials into finished goods will require the preparation of Subsidiary Budgets for *labour* and *machine* time.
- Finally, Subsidiary Budgets need to be prepared for Fixed and Variable Overheads.

A summary of the Master Budget will then look something like:

Sales revenue		X	
Direct costs			
Labour costs			
Machine costs			
Raw materials			
	(X)		
Indirect costs			
Fixed overheads			
Variable overheads	X		
	(X)	(X)	
Profit or loss		X	

B Limiting Factors

Putting the Master Budget together in a way which produces a costed and achievable financial plan, depends upon isolating and then dealing with, any ingredient that could scupper the whole plan from the beginning. This nasty, the Limiting (or limitation) Factor may be, e.g. a shortage of materials required to meet forecast sales demand, a shortfall of relevant quality/quantity of labour or raw materials. There is little point in producing a Master Budget when one part of the jigsaw does not fit. Isolate and deal with that problem part first, in a suitable style to fit the picture.

An immediate chance to practice!

At the end of this chapter you will find an exercise requiring the preparation of a Master and Subsidiary Budget with no Limiting Factor, there are also calculations showing the consequences of dealing with a shortfall in labour availability and raw materials.

C   Preparation of the Budgets

It should by now be clear that the Master Budget is a very important document in the financial success of a business. Put together prudently and carefully; in line with the longer-term strategy of the organisation and used to monitor regularly how actuals are proceeding against the forecast. Internal publication of the approved Master Budget is but a first step in the annual financial cycle.

A key second step, is to take corrective action when things are not proceeding according to plan. You will recall from the depiction of Anthony's hierarchy, that by far the largest part of a business, constitutes staff or the operational level delivering their constituent part of the Master Budget.

How can we best ensure that all operational staff are doing just that?

Your Managerial Level studies will introduce you to the findings of behavioural scientists who have concluded that success in budget delivery is enhanced, if all staff are involved/consulted in its preparation. This participation (democratic or bottom-up) method, contrasts with an autocratic (top-down) diktat of what has been decided behind closed boardroom doors. Of course, senior management takes final decisions and there are circumstances in which autocratic action may be necessary (e.g. at the start of a new business, or where staff are unable to agree or even to prepare a budget). Goal congruence, bringing together corporate and individual workplace aims, gives the best chance of a successful Master Budget delivery.

D   The Budget Committee and Manual

There are two further important ingredients in successful Master Budget planning and delivery. The Budget Committee will perhaps be led by a senior director and will comprise of representatives of functional or divisional heads. In government, this job is carried out by the Chief Secretary to the Treasury, a Cabinet post. The Budget Committee's task is to deal with bids from departments and mould these bids into a Master Budget which commands (publicly at least!), support from those who have to make it work. This task, of course, takes place against any strategic guidance given annually by the Government's "Board of Directors", the Cabinet. The Committee should then meet regularly during the year and carry out the important control function.

The Budget Manual sets out a company's rules and regulations for the budgetary cycle. It should contain details of timing and personal responsibilities and give examples of each document relating to budget preparation and monitoring.

The wider use of the Master Budget

The reader will readily appreciate that the Master Budget (preparing a considered forecast of the next twelve months revenues and spending) effectively produces a draft Profit and Loss Account for the year. If that is accepted, then a Balance Sheet as at the end of the accounting period may also be drafted. So far, our Master Budget has spawned both a forecast Profit and Loss Account and a forecast Balance Sheet, but there is a third and critically important statement to be produced, the Cash Budget. In addition, the business may, having prudently prepared its Master Budget, also have calculated the financial effects of changes in key elements (e.g. sales are 10% up, or there is an expected worldwide rise in the price of raw materials). This process, termed Sensitivity Analysis, introduces the concept of the Flexed Budget.

E   Preparing the Cash Budget

In the medium to longer term, a good and steady return on an investment, is what the shareholder is generally seeking. Students will have learnt early on in their studies, that the use of best estimates of accruals and other devices, can produce an annual profit figure that has no relevance to the amount of cash available. A business can produce a significant increase in its bottom line, at the same time that cash reserves have significantly reduced, or disappeared.

The Master Budget does not take into account the timing of key transactions (sales revenue, the purchase of raw materials, etc.). the accounting concept of "matching", requires transactions to be accounted for in the accounting period to which they relate, but the cash flows relating to those transactions may occur in a different and subsequent period. Thus sales made and accounted for in December, the last month of the financial year, will not see the cash arrive until the following financial year.

In addition, the Master Budget may contain legitimate costs such as provisions, which do not involve cash outflows, whilst the Cash Budget may reflect the purchase of a capital asset which is not directly accounted for in the draft profit and loss account.

Rather like budgets generally, component cash budgeting has two aspects: preparation and control.

In principle, preparation should be relatively straight forward. Cash budgets contain no accruals and are based simply on what flows of money are expected – in or out.

The real purpose in all of this is, having calculated what is expected to be in hand, or not, at the end of a control period – usually a month in the examination room – you then have to decide what action, if any, is needed.

At the end of this chapter, there is an exercise requiring the preparation of a cash budget which then asks you to make decisions on what is revealed therein.

F   Flexed Budget Preparation

Turning now to Flexed or Flexible Budgeting, the Oxford English Dictionary tells us that this is derived from the latin flectere, "to bend".

Secondly, CIMA *Official Terminology* states that Flexed Budgeting involves flexing variable costs from original budgeted levels to the *allowances* permitted for actual volume achieved . . .". This definition takes us right to the heart of cost behaviour, of which there was a lot in Chapter 1.

In putting together our Master Budget, we know that different costs behave in different ways – some are variable, some are fixed, regardless of production levels and some are hybrid (a mixture of the two). The Master Budget is prepared on the basis of a certain level of production and, if during the year, there is a decision to vary that level, then variable and hybrid costs will change. Fixed costs will, of course, remain unaltered, when there is no indication that they will be stepped (e.g. where the increase in production requires additional premises at a higher annual rental).

The CIMA definition of flexed budgeting makes reference to the word "allowances" permitted for the actual volume achieved. "These allowances may – e.g. be expressed as "so much %" or "so much for X units produced".

The following example will explain the calculation and use of these "allowances":

Example 1

A factory has prepared estimates of costs at the following levels of production. For the next 12 months, an 80% output has been prudently forecast, but "what if" budgets of 70% (pessimistic) and 90% (optimistic) have also been drafted. The *task* is to calculate what the forecast total expenditure will be at a production output of 78%.

	70%	80%	90%
	£	£	£
Labour	140,000	160,000	180,000
Materials	595,000	680,000	765,000
Production costs	30,500	32,000	33,500
Advertising	32,000	34,000	36,000
Factory rental	40,000	40,000	40,000
	837,500	946,000	1,054,500

By inspection, the *factory rental* is a fixed cost. We need to test what are the allowances % for the other costs – are they variable or are they hybrid? Using the labour costs at 80% they equate to £2000 for each 1%. This allowance multiplied by 70% and 90% confirms that *labour* is a linear cost. A similar calculation shows us that *Materials* also behave in the same way at £8500 per 1%, but the production costs and advertising expenses do not, so they must be a mixture of fixed and variable costs.

Applying the High–Low calculation (see Chapter 1), tells us that for advertising costs:

At	90% production	36,000
At	70% production	32,000
At	20% increase =	£4,000

Since all of this increase must be variable, a 1% allowance equals £200. At 70%, this totals £14,000 so fixed costs must be £18,000.

For production costs, applying the same High–Low technique gives us a fixed cost of £20,000 and a variable cost, per 1% of £150.

Bringing all of this together, gives a projected cost, at a 78% production level, of:

Labour	156,000
Materials	663,000
Production	31,700
Advertising	33,600
Rental	40,000
	£924,300

The production and use of a Flexed Budget is essential as a feature of the control aspect of budgeting. If production levels have changed, then costs will change and the regular monitoring of progress should take place against the flexed figures, *NOT* against the original budget. In this situation, the original budget is relegated to, perhaps, a role as a valued historical document.

G   Other Types of Budgets

Your CIMA studies work on budgeting methods will concentrate on the three elements of the Master Budget and its subsidiaries. It will also introduce you to other, specialised budgets, so it is appropriate to just mention the principles of:

Zero-based budgets
Rolling budgets
Programme and activity-based budgets

Zero-based budgeting

It is possibly true to say that, in the real world, most Master Budgets are based on an "incremental" approach. The cynic might define such an approach as "take the current year and add on a bit". This might more probably be true of public sector budgeting, generally.

Such an approach, builds in a wish on the part of the budget holder to spend up to the allowance or run the risk of losing some next year. It also does not expose waste and inefficiency which compounds, as the years go by. Zero-based budgeting is defined in CIMA *Official Terminology* as a "method of budgeting that requires all costs to be specifically justified by the benefits expected". It involves starting budget preparation with a clean slate and going back to such basic questions as:

What are we here to do?
What resources will we need to do that?
How much will those resources cost?
When will those resources be needed?

The Master Budget process then starts afresh.

Rolling budgets

Perhaps more accurately termed a "Rolling" or "Continuous Forecast", this provides a "continuously updated forecast, whereby each time actual results are reported, a further forecast period is added and intermediate period forecasts are updated" (CIMA *Official Terminology*).

A Master Budget, prepared for 12 months, will get shorter as each month is completed, but if, when this happens, a further month is added, there is the advantage that there is always a financial plan for 12 months, which keeps people thinking ahead. Against this is a possibility of "budget indigestion" and increasing uncertainty about the future.

Programme and activity-based budgets

Look back at the structure of a Master Budget that we introduced earlier, such headings may be regarded as *subjective*, as they spell out the nature of the expenditure. Many organisations, particularly those which are not in existence for profit, may be more concerned about preparing and controlling their annual budget against specific purposes, or *objectives*, the annual budget of a large local authority, for example, is therefore prepared against specific programmes of work and instead of looking like:

Subjective analysis

		£'000
Employees		92,365
Running expenses	X	
Premises	X	
Supplies and services, etc.	X	29,726
Loan charges		15,479
Capital expenditure		5,000
		£142,570

May be more usefully prepared as follows:

Objective analysis

	£'000
Education	82,360
Social services	15,984
Highways and planning	12,044
Tourism and leisure	8,833
Etc.	23,349
	£142,570

The Capital Budget or capital programme

There is one very specialised budget that gets surprisingly little attention in the CIMA syllabus, but has a significant impact in the real world. Those in the public sector will be familiar with a programme of asset creation – the Capital Budget.

Of course, as we have seen, there are advantages for all businesses in having a costed financial plan of revenues and expenditures for a future period. The Master Budget consumables are revenue items, but businesses need capital assets to assist in the creation of profits and grow. Factories and offices need building; the building needs to be on land and such expenditure takes both time and money. When a new building is completed, it will generate revenue costs, all of which need to be reflected in and financed from the Master Budget.

It is important to realise that the creation of non-current assets, involves revenue financing costs (interest and loan repayments on borrowings, leasing charges, dividends on shareholders funds and a loss of interest if internal reserves are used or a capital cost is charged directly to revenue). Unless a business receives a direct capital grant, with no strings attached, all of the costs of non current assets will need, over time, to be financed from the Master Budget.

A page from a three year Capital Budget, covering the period 2005/08 is shown below. A single sheet summarising a single project. Sheets for all projects, when combined, will form the Capital Budget and, like the Master Budget, will be subject to annual review and revision.

Capital Programme Format

Capital programme 2005/06–2008/09

Details of scheme/project	Analysis of capital cost in summary form
	£ B

Capital cost phasing

	Total	Earlier years	2005–06	2006–07	2007–08	2008–09	Later years	Notes
Capital cost elements in detail								
	B							
Methods of finance								
	B							

H   The Budget and Performance Evaluation

What gets measured gets attention

(Tom Peters)

Let us remind ourselves that budgeting is within the syllabus of Paper P1, which is all about the Evaluation of your Performance. This section of the book would therefore not be complete, without seeing how we can gauge our progress by measuring the proficiency with which we achieve our objectives. Such measurement requires efficient and effective deployment of resources. The CIMA *Official Terminology*, from which this wording is drawn, further advises that measures of performance, may be based on both financial and non-financial information.

Any accountancy student in their early period of studies, will have met "ratio analysis". Since the annual financial statements were prepared, you were required to assess how well the business had done in that period. Accounting text books provided a range of performance measures (ratios) to help assess profitability, efficiency, liquidity, risk and investor ratios (how well shareholders had done). Such ratios were compared with previous periods or, if they were available, industry averages and conclusions drawn. With the exception of the earnings per share ratio, there is no requirement to calculate or publish these performance measures and thus their value was internal, to the business management.

In the Chapter 1 discussion of absorption costing, we met our friends Kaplan and Norton of the Harvard Business School. In that context, they were putting a strong case in favour of basing cost apportionments on the activities which caused them: ABC with its cost pools and cost drivers. These two academics have also developed influential thinking on the measures used to calculate and report on an entity's performance.

The use of traditional financial performance measures is well established, but they suffer from a concentration on the past, with no regard for the future: manipulation and short termism.

Recent thinking has therefore centred not on just financial quantitative measures ("our stock turnover is 22 days: a GPM of 67%") but on non-financial qualitative (expression of service satisfaction for customers) and non-financial qualitative (number of units failing in service: number of passengers carried).

Linking both sets of indicators together, Kaplan and Norton proposed a published balanced picture of overall performance: a balance that represented both good and bad indicators. From this, the concept of a Balance Scorecard has emerged. This emphasises the need to provide the stakeholder "with a set of information, which addresses all relevant areas of performance in an objective and unbiased fashion".

The Harvard academics proposed a concentration on four sets of measures, which they termed "perspectives" (from two Latin terms meaning "through": "to work"):

Customer perspective	–	How do they see us?
Internal business perspective	–	What must we excel at?
Innovation and learning perspective	–	Can we continue to improve and create value?
Financial perspective	–	How do we look to shareholders?

For each perspective, Kaplan and Norton proposed achievement goals and performance measures for each goal. Determining the specific needs to be included in a Balanced Scorecard, requires a business to regularly and continually address three questions:

1 What are the critical success factors?
2 What performance measures can be used to monitor attainment against those factors?
3 What changes must be made to organisational processes in order to facilitate the improvement of performance against those factors?

This chapter contains an exercise requiring you to assess a company's performance on both financial and non-financial indicators. Give it a go!

Performance measurement in the public sector, is much more advanced than that which we have just considered in the private sector. By its very nature, much of the performance information is more widely available and this is certainly true of local government and the NHS. The central government is very good at exhorting others to wider accountability, but is not terribly keen to follow!

Performance measurement in the public sector is centred around the annual published statistics of the CIPFA, or NHS bodies. A very wide range of financial and non-financial unit costs and statistics are published with calculated central and group indicators. Such statistics are key elements in annual central government review (via the Audit Commission) of the performance of individual local authorities.

This mechanism, termed "Benchmarking" is another area of your Managerial Level studies in the P1 Paper. CIMA defines benchmarking as establishing targets and comparators that permits relative levels of performance/underperformance to be identified. It also supports the adoption of identified best practices.

I The Concept of "Beyond Budgeting"

Finally, in this chapter, we look at "Beyond Budgeting", another product (2003) from the Harvard Business School. An independent research collaborative, the Beyond Budgeting Round Table, proposed that, given the present complexity and difficulty of budgeting as mostly practised, it should be abandoned. The BBRT website, lists 10 criticisms of budgeting as developed by Harvard academics:

(a) *Budgets are time consuming and expensive.* Even with the support of computer models, it is estimated that the budgeting process uses up to 20–30% of senior executives' and financial managers' time.

(b) *Budgets provide poor value to users.* Although surveys have shown that some managers feel that budgets give them control, a large majority of financial directors wish to reform the budgetary process, because they feel that finance staff spend too much time on "lower value-added activities".

(c) *Budgets fail to focus on shareholder value.* Most budgets are set on an incremental basis as an acceptable target agreed between the manager and the manager's superior. Managers may be rewarded for achieving their short-term budgets and will not look to the longer term or take risks, for fear of affecting their own short-term results.

(d) *Budgets are too rigid and prevent fast response.* Although most organisations do update and revise their budgets at regular intervals as the budget period proceeds the process if often too slow compared with the pace at which the external environment is changing.

(e) *Budgets protect rather than reduce costs.* Once a manager has an authorised budget he can spend that amount of resource without further authorisation. A "use it or lose it" mentality often develops so that managers will incur cost unnecessarily. This happens especially towards the end of the budget period in the expectation that managers will not be permitted to carry forward any unused resource into the budget for next period.

(f) *Budgets stifle production and strategy innovation.* The focus on achieving the budget discourages managers from taking risks in case this has adverse effects on their short-term performance. Managers do not have the freedom to respond to changing customer needs in a fast changing market because the activity they would need to undertake is not authorised in their budget.

(g) *Budgets focus on sales targets rather than customer satisfaction.* The achievement of short term sales forecasts becomes the focus of most organisations. However this does not necessarily result in customer satisfaction. The customer may be sold something *inappropriate to their needs*, as in recent years in the UK financial services industry. Alternatively, if a manager has already met the sales target for a particular period they might try to *delay sales to the next period*, in order to give themselves a "head start" towards achieving the target for the next period. Furthermore, there is an incentive towards the end of a period, if a manager feels that the sales target is not going to be achieved for the period to *delay sales until the next period*, and thus again have a head start towards achieving the target for the next period. All of these actions, focusing on sales targets rather than customer satisfaction, will have a detrimental effect on the organisation in the longer term.

(h) *Budgets are divorced from strategy.* Most organisations monitor the monthly results against the short-term budget for the month. What is needed instead is a system of monitoring the longer item progress against the organisation's strategy.

(i) *Budgets reinforce a dependency culture.* The process of planning and budgeting with a framework devolved from senior management perpetuates a culture of dependency. Traditional budgeting systems, operated on a centralised basis, do not encourage a culture of *personal responsibility*.

(j) *Budgets lead to unethical behaviour.* For example, we have seen in this chapter a number of opportunities for dysfunctional behaviour such as *building slack into the budget* in order to create an easier target for achievement.

Underlying these issues are thoughts on the development of management accounting generally. The principles of JIT and kaizen (described in Chapter 1) could also apply to budgeting, with a greater empowerment of relevant Tactical and Operational level staffs. Such employees could be more adaptive and flexible, with the ability to concentrate on benchmarks and performance measures, rather than purely on cost control. Clearly, closer team working would be an essential aspect for the success of such an arrangement.

Item (h) above, is very relevant to a new CIMA initiative. Over the past 2 years, CIMA has developed the CIMA Strategic Scorecard, as a way to support Boards fulfilling their duty to oversee strategy. There is a lengthy quality article, by the Institute's governance specialist, Gillian Lees, in *Financial Management* for May 2007.

Revision Questions

1 Preparing Master and Subsidiary Budgets with no limiting factors

Sibelius Ltd manufactures two products, a Tuonela (T) and a Kalavela (K) which are used music reproduction. The company is about to prepare a master budget for the year commencing 1 July 2005 and the following relevant information is available for this purpose.

Budgeted sales   T 22,000 @ £180 per unit
                             K 14,000 @ £195 per unit

	Opening inventories	Closing inventories
Finished goods	200T and 100K	500T and 100K
Raw material A	4500 kg	4000 kg
Raw material B	2900 kg	2900 kg

Each finished unit requires:

	T	K
Material A @ £1.60 kg	10 kg	12 kg
Material B @ £2.10 kg	8 kg	8 kg
Labour hours @ £6 per hour	9	11
Machine hours		
Shop A @ £1.10 per hour	4	6
Shop B @ 52p per hour	4	4

Production overheads

V £1.50 per machine hour
F £0.50 per machine hour

Requirement
To produce all relevant subsidiary budgets and a Master Budget in the style of a Profit and loss account, for the year commencing 1 July 2005.

2 Preparing Master and Subsidiary Budgets with labour and materials as limiting factors.

This question builds on the Master Budget of Sibelius Ltd above.

A problem has occurred! Due to a local war in a distant country, there is a worldwide, but temporary, shortage of raw material A. There is still plenty of material B available. Only 350,000 kg of material A can be made available and that will cost £2/kg. Sibelius could possibly use a substitute material, but has ruled this out on the basis of maintaining standards.

It has therefore decided to redraw its budgets for the next year, on the basis of accepting all the material A that can be made available. It is still the company's intention to maximise its profit in the next financial year.

Requirement
Prepare the new subsidiary and Master Budgets for the next financial year, on the basis of the changed circumstances.

3   Preparing a Cash Budget

Vaughan Williams plc manufactures and sells a single product called the "Wasp". Each unit sells for £100 and requires 3 kg of Snibbo @ £5 kg and 2 hours of labour @ £20 per hour. You have been asked to assist in the preparation of the next Cash Budget, for which the following information has been made available.

Sales in months	1–6000
	2–7000
	3–7500
	4–8000
	5–8000
	6–8000
Opening inventories:	Snibbo 500 kg
	Completed Wasps 1500

Inventories of finished goods at the end of each month are 10% of the expected sales for the following month.

Raw materials are paid for in the following month and labour costs are paid for in the current month.

70% of expected sales revenues are received in the month of sale; 20% in the following month and 10% in the month after that.

A new machine will be delivered in month 2 at a cost of £41,500 and will be paid for in month 4.

Variable overheads are 2% of each month's sales and monthly fixed overheads are £15,000. Both are paid in the month.

The rent of a small factory building is £500 in month 1 and payments increase by 2% each month.

Monthly depreciation on plant and equipment, included in fixed overheads is £1500.

A bank overdraft facility of £10,000 is available and the cash in hand at the beginning of month 1 is £8200.

Requirements
   (a) Prepare a cash budget for months 2, 3 and 4.
   (b) Comment on the month-end position revealed by your budget.

4   Performance Assessment Exercise

Hummel Ltd, a world famous maker and seller of quality widgets, is a great advocate of the Balanced Scorecard, as a method of reporting performance to its stakeholders. Each year, its annual report contains an appendix of financial and non-financial performance indicators.

The current annual report, for 2004, contains the following 3-year summary of those indicators:

	2002	2003	2004
Gross profit margin (%)	65	67	64
Net profit margin (%)	28	31	28
Creditor payment (days)	57	56	54
Debtor payment (days)	44	49	41
Stock turnover (days)	34	34	33
Earnings per share (p)	7.5	8.1	8.6
Staff turnover (%)	5	11	13
Tender success rate (%)	69	66	71

Requirement
As an investment analyst, write a brief note on the picture revealed by these indicators, for the financial pages of the *Daily Bugle*.

5   Mahler plc is currently considering a statement of production performance for the month of January 2005. During the current financial year, its average level of production is 30,000 units per month, but actual production can vary

significantly from this average, due to the weather. The average level of monthly costs (in £'000) and the actual figures for January 2005, are shown below:

Production costs	Monthly average (30,000)	Jan 2005 actual (22,500)
Labour	160,000	119,925
Materials	234,000	175,500
Depreciation	27,000	27,000
Production overheads	75,000	64,500
Other overheads	111,000	94,500
Totals	607,000	481,425

Requirements
(a) Prepare flexed monthly budgets at both 28,000 and 34,000 units of production.

6   Having prepared a prudent budget for the new financial year, the Board of Elgar Ltd, a wine importer, is quite content to do without monthly, or any, control reports. As the new Financial Director, you are told that "we have always waited until the end of the year to see how things have gone and they have always been better than expected, but let us know what you think".

Requirement
Prepare a report for the Board on the need for, and the importance of, budgetary control stressing the criteria that periodical control reports should possess.

7   What benefits does the preparation of a Capital Budget or programme, offer (a) to the forward planning of a business and (b) to the preparation of the annual master budget?

8   The annual master budget of Grieg plc has, for the past 20 years, since the company was founded, been produced on an incremental basis. The Board has noticed a reduction in profits in the past 3 years.

Requirement
Explain how incrementalism in budget preparation can impact on annual profits and list the benefits of an alternative method of budget preparation.

Solutions to Revision Questions

1

1 Prepare the Sales Budget

	T	K	Total
Units	22,000	14,000	36,000
Value (£)	3,960,000	2,730,000	6,690,000

2 But what do we need to produce?

Sales Budget requires	22,000	14,000
Stock increase	300	–
Total production	**22,300**	**14,000**

3 How much material (kg) will this require?

		Material A		Material B
To produce T	22,300 × 10	223,000	22,300 × 8	178,400
To produce K	14,000 × 12	168,000	14,000 × 8	112,000
Total (kg)		**391,000**		**290,400**
Stock movement		(500)		–
To purchase		**390,500**		**290,400**
This will cost (£)		**£624,800**		**£609,840**

4 How much will we need to spend on labour?

T will require 22,300 × 9 hours	200,700
K will require 14,000 × 11 hours	154,000

A total of 354,700 hours at a total cost of (×£6) = **£2,128,200**

5 How many machine hours will we need?

		Shop A		Shop B
For T	22,300 × 4	89,200	22,300 × 4	89,200
For K	14,000 × 6	84,000	14,000 × 4	56,000
		173,200		**145,200**

A total of **318,400** hours

6   What about the total cost of overheads we will incur?

Variable cost	318,400 hours × £1.50 =	477,600
Fixed cost	318,400 hours × 0.50 =	159,200
Total		**£636,800**

7   Preparing the Master Budget (P and L Account)

This can now be commenced, but we have some closing stocks to consider. That means we need to work out the values of our year end stocks of both raw materials and finished goods, to enable calculation of the cost of sales.

(a)   Raw materials

A	4000 kg @ £1.60	6,400
B	2900 kg @ £2.10	6,090
		£12,490

(b)   Finished goods

		T		K
Materials				
A 10 kg		16.0	12 kg	19.2
B 8 kg		16.8	8 kg	16.8
		32.8		36.0
Wages	9 hours	54.0	11 hours	66.0
Overheads	8 hours	16.0	10 hours	20.0
Total unit cost		**102.8**		**122.0**
Units of finished goods		500		100
Total value		**£51,400**		**£12,200**

Calculating the cost of sales

Opening stocks			
Raw materials	13,290*		
Finished goods	32,760**		46,050
Raw materials			1,234,600
Labour			2,124,000
Overheads			648,000
			4,052,690
Closing stocks as (a)			(76,090)
Cost of sales			**£3,976,600**
Raw materials	A	4500 × £1.60	7,200
	B	2900 × £2.10	6,090
			£13,290*
Finished goods	T	200 × £102.8	20,560
	K	100 × £122.0	12,200
			£32,760**

Profit and loss account

	Sales	6,690,000
	Cost of Sales	3,976,600
		2,713,400
	Administration overheads (say)	(100,000)
Profit		**£2,613,400**

2

Here we have the need to produce a Master Budget when there is a shortage of raw material A. This means that we do not have sufficient material A to manufacture all the finished goods that we require for the Production Budget, at present 39,500 kg. The key wording in this question is "maximises profit". As Sibelius makes two products, such raw materials as we can get, need to be concentrated on the product which gives the bigger contribution per unit. "The bigger the contribution, the bigger the profit!"

At present, individual contributions are T £81.20 and K £78.00. Since Tuonelas give the bigger contribution, Sibelius should make up to the production demand of T and then make as many K as it can before the balance of material A runs out.

3

(a) Cash Budget
     The question calls for a three month forecast only, but the model answer shows the whole period. This breaches the exam. rule that you should do what you are asked to do and not what you think you should do!

	1	2	3	4	5	6
Sales revenue	420,000	610,000	725,000	780,000	795,000	800,000
Raw materials	–	75,500	105,750	113,250	120,000	120,000
Labour	208,000	282,000	302,000	320,000	320,000	320,000
New machine	–	–	–	41,500	–	–
Variable overheads	120	140	150	160	160	160
Fixed overheads	13,500	13,500	13,500	13,500	13,500	13,500
Rent	500	510	520	530	540	550
	222,120	371,650	421,920	488,940	454,200	454,210
Net cash flow	197,880	238,350	303,080	291,060	340,800	345,790
Opening balance	8,200	206,080	444,430	747,510	1,038,570	1,379,370
Closing balance	**206,080**	**444,430**	**747,510**	**1,038,570**	**1,379,370**	**1,725,160**

Calculation of labour and raw material costs

	1	2	3	4	5	6
Sales	6,000	7,000	7,500	8,000	8,000	8,000
+Closing stock	700	750	800	800	800	800
−Opening stock	1,500	700	750	800	800	800
Units required	**5,200**	**7,050**	**7,550**	**8,000**	**8,000**	**8,000**
Material required	15,600 kg	21,150	22,650	24,000	24,000	24,000
Opening stock	(500)					
Total required	**15,100**	**21,150**	**22,650**	**24,000**	**24,000**	**24,000**
Material cost ×£5	75,500	105,750	113,250	120,000	120,000	120,000
Labour cost ×£40	208,000	282,000	302,000	320,000	320,000	320,000

(b) This is a most healthy position, with the new machine making barely an impact! If there is no proposal for major expenditure in the near future, then there should be some serious (and profitable) investing in a good cash deposit account.

4

This is a report for the local "freebie", so we can dispense with the formal structure that was required for our Chairman, in another question. The summary provided contains both good and bad news, as well as both financial and non financial indicators. The key words in answering the question are "Balanced Scorecard", so we need to structure the answer around the four perspectives (see page 171).

Customer perspective

The tender success rate has increased in the past year, after a slight reduction so we assume that potential future customers are happy to take our widgets. We are also paying our bills promptly, which should please our raw material suppliers.

Internal business perspective

The GPM is steady, but there must be concern over the decline in the NPM, indicating the need for costs to be closely scrutinised and reduced. The inventory turnover is also steady and good for this type of business (all stock cleared monthly).

Innovation perspective

The staff turnover rate is, on the face of it, a very worrying trend. The reasons for this need to be well established and addressed as a matter of urgency.

Financial perspective

Earnings per share are almost 15% up over the review period, which should keep our stakeholders happy.

Learn from the excellent precept of Occam's Razor in Appendix A (qv). You do not have too much material, or detail, to use in preparing your report, so spell out the basics, keep it simple and don't go looking for trouble.

5

The application of the "allowances" (see page 165), to test the type of production expense is very relevant in this High–Low question.

Production cost	Type	28,000 units	34,000 units
Labour	Linear	149,324	181,322
Material	Linear	218,400	265,200
Depreciation	Fixed	27,000	27,000
Production overheads	Hybrid	72,200	80,600
Other overheads	Hybrid	106,600	119,800
Totals (£)		**573,524**	**673,922**

6

This report requires a formal structure, centring around a definition of budgetary control. This may be defined as the process by which financial control is exercised within a business. The annual Master (Tactical) Budget, is a planned and costed step along the longer-term road to the achievement of Strategic aims. As such, it is an important and considered, which shapes the daily work of all within the organisation. Regular monitoring by comparing actuals with the budgetary provision, enables management to see when things are not proceeding according to the annual plan. Appropriate corrective action may then be taken.

If circumstances change materially since the original budget was prepared (e.g. sales are clearly going to be much more than estimated) then a new, flexed, budget becomes the document against which (monthly) control reports are prepared and subsequently actioned.

7

(a) An example of a Capital Budget sheet is shown on page 169. The intention is that each scheme or project, has a separate sheet and then all completed sheets are summarised and bound. The forward planning of a business demands, on the part of directors, a strategic vision of both direction and time. The creation of major non current assets, either by acquisition or by building, takes time and a lot of money. It cannot all be done, or financed at once, so capital schemes are prioritised and these priorities are reflected in the capital programme timing. The capital budget will show volumes of capital expenditure for each year of the programme and broad indications of how such expenditure will be funded.

(b) A detailed capital programme will show timings of proposals – commencement and completion – and the flow of capital monies. Unless there is an outright capital grant, all capital financing costs will need to be met from the annual master budget. As new facilities come on stream, there will be the new costs of labour, materials and overheads to meet as well as loan repayments and leasing costs. New expenditure may be financed in whole or part by the sale or closure of existing facilities.

8

An incremental budget is based on using a previous period budget, or actual performance, as a start with incremental amounts added for the new budget period. These incremental sums may often take the form of allowances for inflation (e.g. a 2.5% pay increase) added to the budget provision for the current year. This approach may not take into account changed circumstances, or operating conditions and will thus "build in" budget provision in the past which is not required for the future. Over time, this process of "adding on a bit to last year's figure" will conceal waste, inefficiency and an unwillingness to challenge established procedures.

A main alternative, which is designed to challenge established procedures, is zero-based budgeting (see page 166), in which a manager is required to prepare a budget from scratch and on the assumption that there is no commitment to spend any money. Thus each aspect of a budget heading, or allowance needs to be justified afresh against the overall plans of the business.

Appendix A: Glossary of Terms, (those not in the CIMA *Official Terminology*)

Audit	From the Latin "audire" – to hear, from times when accounts were examined orally.
BODMAS	Brackets, Other (e.g. roots), Division, Multiplication, Addition, Subtraction, the order in which arithmetical calculations are to be carried out e.g. $2 \times 6 + 3 = 15$ and not 18. (see page 125)
Congruence	From the Latin "congruere" – to run together. (see page 170)
Corporate Governance	The manner in which directors carry out their stewardship responsibilities as managers of a company.
Exposure Draft	Or FRED – an early draft of the wording of a proposed Accounting Standard, widely circulated for comments.
Iterative	From the Latin "iterare" – again
Occam's Razor	The principle that, in explaining something, no more assumptions should be made than are absolutely necessary (e.g. in suggesting why standard costing variances may be (A) or (F))
Opinion	From the Latin "opinari" – think, believe. From audit work undertaken, the auditor's view of the truth and fairness of financial statements.
Principles-Based Standards	A set of principles to be applied to the preparation of financial statements, which give flexibility to use judgement in deciding the most appropriate treatment of items. As opposed to prescriptive standards,which are inflexible, detailed rules.
Reciprocal Method	From the Latin "reciprocus" – back and forward as with service cost centre allocation (see page 19)
Recognised Supervisory Body	A body established under the Companies Act 1989 to maintain and enforce rules as to the qualification of company auditors and the conduct of audit work. (see page 97)

Regulatory Framework	The whole set of statutory, mandatory and guidance documents issued by official bodies, to ensure the quality and reliability of published financial statements.
"RRCU"	The four qualities or "qualitative characteristics" that a company's Annual Report should contain. Relevance, Reliability, Comparability, Understandability.
Stewardship	Competent management of another's property, e.g. a basic duty of a Board of Directors.
Stochastic	From the Greek "stochastikos" – random.
True and Fair View	The statutory requirement (Companies Act 1985), for an unqualified audit Opinion. True means relatively factually correct (e.g. the best available considered judgement of the economic life of an asset has been made). Fair implies reasonable, impartial and without bias, e.g. what is a reasonable size for a provision?
Treasury Management	The machinery and procedures in an organisation for the efficient management of financing resources and investments.
Yellow Book	The "Listing Rules" of the London Stock Exchange, which require the directors of UK-listed companies to disclose certain corporate governance information in an annual report. Such disclosures to be the subject of review by auditors.

Appendix B: Useful Websites

CIMA – UK Head Office	www.cimaglobal.com
Exemptions	www.cimaglobal.com/exemptions2
Tuition Colleges	www.cimaglobal.com/colleges2
Examination Centres	www.cimaglobal.com/examcentres2
Past Papers	www.cimaglobal.com/studyresources2
Fees	www.cimaglobal.com/fees2

Accounting Standards Board	www.asb.org.uk/asb
Auditing Practices Board	www.asb.org.uk/apb
Financial Reporting Council	www.asb.org.uk
International Accounting Standards Board	www.iasb.org

| Publishers | www.cimapublishing.com |
| | www.books.elsevier.com |

Appendix C: IAS 1
Presentation of Financial Information (revised December 2003)

Key points

The objective of IAS 1 is to prescribe the basis for presentation of general purpose financial statements. It sets out the overall framework and responsibilities for the presentation of financial statements, guidelines for their structure, and minimum requirements for the content of financial statements. IAS 1 applies to all general purpose financial statements prepared in accordance with International Financial Reporting Standards. General purpose financial statements are defined as those intended to serve users who do not have the authority to demand financial reports tailored for their own needs.

Content of financial statements

The financial statements should comprise the following:

1 Balance sheet
2 Income statement
3 Statement of changes in equity or statement of non-owner changes in equity
4 Cash flow statement
5 Explanatory notes including a summary of significant accounting policies.

There is no prescribed standard format, although examples of the minimum headings are provided in the Appendix. It does, however, set out minimum disclosures to be made on the face of the financial statements as well as in the notes. For example, an analysis of income and expenditure using a classification based on their nature or function must be disclosed. The standard also requires comparatives to be provided for all items unless a particular accounting standard specifically exempts that requirement.

The reporting currency should generally be that of the country in which the enterprise is domiciled. If a different reporting currency is adopted or a change in reporting currency made, then the reasons must be disclosed.

A reporting enterprise complying with the requirements of IFRSs is considered as providing a fair presentation of the financial statements. A statement that the financial statements comply with IFRSs and SIC interpretations is required. No statement is now permitted stating that compliance with IFRSs has been undertaken with certain specified exemptions. Full compliance is essential.

Overall considerations

Fair presentation and compliance with IFRSs

Financial statements should present fairly the financial position, performance and cash flows of the entity, and the entity should provide an explicit and unreserved statement that the statements are in compliance with IFRSs.

Inappropriate policies are not rectified either by disclosure or by notes.

Entities can, in rare circumstances, depart from an IFRS (if it is regarded as misleading), but the following must be disclosed in those cases:

- management has concluded that the financial statements give a fair presentation;
- that it has complied with IFRSs etc. except from a particular requirement to achieve fair presentation;
- the title of the IFRS, nature of departure and why the normal treatment was not adopted; and
- the financial impact for each period of the departure.

If departure is not permitted, the entity should reduce the perceived misleading aspects by disclosing:

- the title of the standard, the nature of issue and the reason why it was misleading;
- the adjustments management has concluded would be appropriate.

Going concern Management must assess the ability of an entity to continue as a going concern. If there are doubts over that concept, disclosure should be made of the underlying uncertainties; however, if it is more serious, the financial statements should be prepared on a break up basis but that fact must be disclosed.

Offsetting Assets and liabilities and income and expenses should not be offset unless required or permitted by a standard or SIC.

Comparative information This should be disclosed for the previous period for all amounts disclosed in the financial statements. If the current period has been reclassified so should the comparatives, unless that is impracticable. If practical, the following should be disclosed:

- the nature of the reclassification;
- the amount of each item or class of items reclassified; and
- the reason for the reclassification.

Where it is found to be impractical, the following should be disclosed:

- the reason for not reclassifying; and
- the nature of the adjustments that would have been made.

Structure and content

Identification of the financial statements The financial statements should be clearly identified and distinguished from other information in the same published document.

Each component should be clearly identified. In addition, the following information should be displayed prominently:

- the name of the reporting entity and any change from the preceding year;
- whether the statements cover an individual or group of entities;
- the balance sheet date or period covered;
- the presentation currency;
- the level of rounding adopted.

Reporting period There is a presumption that financial statements will be prepared annually, at a minimum. If the annual reporting period changes and financial statements are prepared for a different period, the entity should disclose the reason for the change and a warning that the corresponding amounts shown may not be comparable.

Balance sheet

The standard specifies minimum headings to be presented on the face of the balance sheet, and guidance is provided for the identification of additional line items.

Entities should present the balance sheet by separating current from non-current assets and liabilities unless a presentation based on liquidity provides information that is more reliable and relevant. If the latter, assets and liabilities must be presented broadly in order of their liquidity (or reverse order), without a current/non-current distinction.

In either case, if an asset/liability category combines amounts that will be received/settled after twelve months with assets/liabilities that will be received/settled within twelve months, note disclosure is required that separates the longer-term amounts from the amounts due to be received/settled within twelve months.

Current assets

An asset is classified as current when it satisfies any of the following criteria:

- it is expected to be realised in the entity's normal operating cycle; or
- it is held primarily for trade; or
- it is expected to be realised within twelve months; or
- it is cash or a cash equivalent.

Non-current assets incorporate tangible, intangible and financial assets of a long-term nature.

Current liabilities

A liability is classified as current when it satisfies any of the following criteria:

- it is expected to be settled in the entity's normal operating cycle; or
- it is held primarily for trade; or
- it is due to be settled within twelve months; or
- the entity does not have an unconditional right to defer settlement for at least twelve months.

Information to be presented on the face of the balance sheet

As a minimum, the following should be disclosed on the face of the balance sheet:

- property, plant and equipment;
- investment property;
- intangible assets;
- financial assets;
- investments accounted under the equity method;
- biological assets;
- inventories;
- trade and other receivables;
- cash and cash equivalents;
- trade and other payables;
- provisions;
- financial liabilities;
- current tax;
- deferred tax;
- minority interest;
- capital and reserves.

Additional items may be presented, if relevant to an understanding of the entity's financial position. Deferred tax may not be reclassified as a current asset/liability if an entity adopts the current/non-current approach.

The standard does not prescribe the order or format of the balance sheet – it is merely a list of items warranting separate disclosure.

Information to be presented either on the face of the balance sheet or in the notes
Further subclassifications may be provided in the notes or on the face of the balance sheet:

- for each class of share capital: number of authorised shares, number of issued shares, par value per share, reconciliation of number outstanding over the year, any rights or restrictions, any treasury shares held and any shares reserved for options including terms and conditions;
- a description of the nature and purpose of each reserve.

Any entity without share capital or a trust should provide equivalent information to the above.

Income statement
All items of income and expense recognised in a period should be included in the income statement unless a standard or SIC requires otherwise (e.g. IAS 8, 16, 21).

IAS 1 specifies the minimum headings that must be presented on the face of the income statement, and provides guidance for the identification of additional line items. There is no particular format or order of presentation mandated.

Information to be presented on the face of the income statement
As a minimum, the following should be disclosed on the face of the income statement for the period:

- revenue;
- finance costs;
- share of profit/loss of associates and joint ventures;
- pre-tax gain or loss recognised on the disposal of assets or settlement of liabilities attributable to discontinuing operations;
- tax expense;
- profit or loss.

The following items should be disclosed on the face of the income statement as allocations of profit:

- minority interest;
- profit/loss attributable to equity holders of the parent.

Additional items should be presented when such presentation is relevant to understanding the entity's financial performance. However, extraordinary items are no longer permitted to be disclosed in the statement or in the notes.

Information to be presented either on the face of the income statement or in the notes
Where material, the nature and amount of income and expenses should be disclosed separately. Examples include inventory writedowns, restructurings, disposals of plant etc., discontinuing operations, litigation settlements, etc.

Income and expenses should not be offset unless another IAS requires or permits such offset, or the amounts to be offset arise from the same events and are not material.

Expenses should be analysed either by nature (raw materials, staff costs, depreciation etc.) or by function (cost of sales, selling, administration, etc.) either on the face of the income statement or in the notes. If an entity categorises by function, additional information on the nature of expenses, including depreciation, amortisation and employee benefit expense, should be disclosed. The choice of method should the one that provides the most reliable and relevant information to the entity.

An entity should disclose, either on the face of the income statement or the statement of changes in equity, or in the notes, the amount of dividends recognised as distributions to equity holders during the period, and the related amount per share.

Statement of changes in equity
IAS 1 requires the presentation of a statement of changes in equity as a separate component of the financial statements, showing:

- the profit or loss for the period;
- each item of income or expense, and gain or loss, that is recognised directly in equity and the total of those items; and
- the effects of changes in accounting policies or material errors in accordance with IAS 8.

Either within this statement or separately in the notes, the entity is required to disclose:

- capital transactions;
- the balance of accumulated profits at the beginning and at end of the period, and the movements for the period; and
- a reconciliation between the carrying amount of each class of equity capital, share premium and each reserve at the beginning and end of the period, disclosing each movement.

Cash flow statement
IAS 1 refers to IAS 7 *Cash Flow Statements* (1992) for presenting the cash flow statement.

Notes

Structure
The notes should:

- present information about the basis of preparation of the financial statements and the specific accounting policies adopted;
- disclose information required by IFRSs not included on the face of the primary statements; and
- provide additional information that is relevant to understanding the financial statements.

Notes should be presented in a systematic manner, and each item cross-referenced to the primary statements.

Accounting policies
The notes, as a minimum, should disclose the significant accounting policies adopted; narrative descriptions or detailed analyses of items shown on the face of the financial statements; information required or encouraged by other IASs; and other disclosures necessary for an understanding and the fair presentation of the financial statements.

The accounting policies section should describe the measurement basis adopted in preparing the financial statements and each specific accounting policy that is necessary for an understanding of the financial statements.

An entity should disclose, in the summary of significant accounting policies or other notes, the judgements, apart from those involving estimates, that management has made in the process of applying the entity's accounting policies that have the most significant effect on the amounts recognised in the financial statements.

Key sources of estimation uncertainty An entity should disclose in the notes information about the key assumptions concerning the future and other key sources of estimation uncertainty at the balance sheet date that have a significant risk of causing a material adjustment to the carrying amounts of assets and liabilities. Details of their nature and carrying amount at the balance sheet date should also be provided.

Other disclosures
In the notes, disclosures should include:

- dividends proposed or declared before the accounts have been authorised and related amounts per share;
- the amount of any cumulative preference dividends not recognised.

If not disclosed elsewhere, the following should be included:

- the domicile and legal form of the entity; country of incorporation and address of registered office if different from the principal place of business;
- a description of the nature of the entity's operations and principal activities;
- the name of the parent and ultimate parent of the group.

Review of performance and financial position IAS 1 encourages the management to include a review of the financial performance and position of the enterprise and to discuss the principal uncertainties that it faces. Such a review would be similar in content to the Management Discussion & Analysis (MD&A) in the United States, and the Operating and Financial Review (OFR) in the United Kingdom and Ireland. The review would include a discussion of dividend policy, changes in the operating environment, funding and risk management policies.

SIC 29 Disclosure – Service Concession Arrangements Comprehensive disclosures are required in respect of service concession arrangements both in the financial statements of the concession operator and the concession provider. These are similar to the rules on PFI contracts that are covered in the ASB's accounting standard on reporting substance (FRS 5).

Guidance on implementing IAS 1

This guidance accompanies, but is not part of, IAS 1.

Illustrative financial statement structure

The standard sets out the components of financial statements and minimum requirements for disclosure on the face of the balance sheet and the income statement as well as for the presentation of changes in equity. It also describes further items that may be presented either on the face of the relevant financial statement or in the notes. This guidance provides simple examples of ways in which the requirements of the standard for the presentation of the balance sheet, income statement and changes in equity might be met. The order of presentation and the descriptions used for line items should be changed, when necessary, in order to achieve a fair presentation in each entity's particular circumstances.

The illustrative balance sheet shows one way in which a balance sheet distinguishing between current and non-current items may be presented. Other formats may be equally appropriate, provided the distinction is clear.

Two income statements are provided, to illustrate the alternative classifications of income and expenses, by nature and by function. Two possible approaches to presenting changes in equity are also illustrated.

The examples are not intended to illustrate all aspects of IFRSs; nor do they comprise a complete set of financial statements, which would also include a cash flow statement, a summary of significant accounting policies and other explanatory notes.

Part A – Illustrative financial statement structure

XYZ GROUP – BALANCE SHEET AS AT 31 DECEMBER 2002

(in thousands of currency units)

	2002	2001
ASSETS		
Non-current assets		
Property, plant and equipment	X	X
Goodwill	X	X
Other intangible assets	X	X
Investments in associates	X	X
Available-for-sale investments	X	X
	X	X

Current assets

Inventories	X	X
Trade receivables	X	X
Other current assets	X	X
Cash and cash equivalents	X̲	X̲
	X̲	X̲
Total assets	X̲	X̲

EQUITY AND LIABILITIES
Equity attributable to equity holders
of the parent

Share capital	X	X
Other reserves	X	X
Retained earnings	X̲	X̲
	X	X
Minority interest	X̲	X̲
Total equity	X̲	X̲

Non-current liabilities

Long-term borrowings	X	X
Deferred tax	X	X
Long-term provisions	X̲	X̲
Total non-current liabilities	X̲	X̲

Current liabilities

Trade and other payables	X	X
Short-term borrowings	X	X
Current portion of long-term borrowings	X	X
Current tax payable	X	X
Short-term provisions	X̲	X̲
Total liabilities	X̲	X̲
Total equity and liabilities	X̲	X̲

XYZ GROUP – INCOME STATEMENT FOR THE YEAR ENDED 31 DECEMBER 2002

(illustrating the classification of expenses by function)
(in thousands of currency units)

	2002	2001
Revenue	X	X
Cost of sales	(X)	(X)
Gross profit	X	X
Other income	X	X
Distribution costs	(X)	(X)
Administrative expenses	(X)	(X)
Other expenses	(X)	(X)
Finance costs	(X)	(X)
Share of profit of associates	X	X
Profit before tax	X	X
Income tax expense	(X)	(X)
Profit for the period	X	X
Attributable to:		
Equity holders of the parent	X	X
Minority interest	X	X
	X	X

XYZ GROUP – INCOME STATEMENT FOR THE YEAR ENDED 31 DECEMBER 2002

(illustrating the classification of expenses by nature)

(in thousands of currency units)

	2002	2001
Revenue	X	X
Other income	X	X
Changes in inventories of finished goods and work in progress	(X)	X
Work performed by the entity and capitalised	X	X
Raw material and consumables used	(X)	(X)
Employee benefits expense	(X)	(X)
Depreciation and amortisation expense	(X)	(X)
Impairment of property, plant and equipment	(X)	(X)
Other expenses	(X)	(X)
Finance costs	(X)	(X)
Share of profit of associates	X̲	X̲
Profit before tax	X	X
Income tax expense	(X̲)	(X̲)
Profit for the period	X̲	X̲
Attributable to:		
Equity holders of the parent	X	X
Minority interest	X̲	X̲
	X̲	X̲

XYZ GROUP – STATEMENT OF CHANGES IN EQUITY FOR THE YEAR ENDED 31 DECEMBER 2002

(in thousands of currency units)

	Share capital	Other reserves	Translation reserve	Retained earnings	Total	Minority interest	Total equity
					Attributable to equity holders of the parent		
Balance at 31 December 2001	X	X	(X)	X	X	X	X
Changes in accounting policy				(X)	(X)	(X)	(X)
Restated balance	X	X	(X)	X	X	X	X
Changes in equity for 2002							
Gain on property revaluation		X			X	X	X
Available-for-sale investments:							
Valuation gains/(losses) taken to equity		(X)			(X)		(X)
Transferred to profit or loss on sale		(X)			(X)		(X)
Cash flow hedges:							
Gains/(losses) taken to equity		X			X	X	X
Transferred to profit or loss for the period		X			X	X	X
Transferred to initial carrying amount of hedged items		(X)			(X)		(X)
Exchange differences on translating foreign operations			(X)		(X)	(X)	(X)

	1	2	3	4	5	6	7
Tax on items taken directly to or transferred from equity		(X)	(X)		(X)	(X)	(X)
Net income recognised directly in equity		X	(X)		X	X	X
Profit for the period				X	X	X	X
Total recognised income and expense for the period		X	(X)	X	X	X	X
Dividends				(X)	(X)	(X)	(X)
Issue of share capital	X				X		X
Equity share options issued		X			X		X
Balance at 31 December 2002 carried forward	X	X	(X)	X	X	X	X

XYZ GROUP – STATEMENT OF RECOGNISED INCOME AND EXPENSE FOR THE YEAR ENDED 31 DECEMBER 2002

(in thousands of currency units)

	2002	2001
Gain/(loss) on revaluation of properties	(X)	X
Available-for-sale investments:		
Valuation gains/(losses) taken to equity	(X)	(X)
Transferred to profit or loss on sale	X	(X)
Cash flow hedges:		
Gains/(losses) taken to equity	X	X
Transferred to profit or loss for the period	(X)	X
Transferred to the initial carrying amount of hedged items	(X)	(X)
Exchange differences on translation of foreign operations	(X)	(X)
Tax on items taken directly to or transferred from equity	X	(X)
Net income recognised directly in equity	(X)	X
Profit for the period	X	X
Total recognised income and expense for the period	X	X

Attributable to:

Equity holders of the parent	X	X
Minority interest	<u>X</u>	<u>X</u>
	<u><u>X</u></u>	<u><u>X</u></u>

Effect of changes in accounting policy:

Equity holders of the parent	(X)
Minority interest	<u>(X)</u>
	<u><u>(X)</u></u>

Appendix D: Formulae

Descriptive statistics

Arithmetic Mean

$$\bar{x} = \frac{\sum x}{n}, \quad \bar{x} = \frac{\sum fx}{\sum f} \quad \text{(frequency distribution)}$$

Standard Deviation

$$SD = \sqrt{\frac{\sum(x - \bar{x})^2}{n}}, \quad SD = \sqrt{\frac{\sum fx^2}{\sum f} - \bar{x}^2} \quad \text{(frequency distribution)}$$

Time series

Additive Model

$$\text{Series} = \text{Trend} + \text{Seasonal} + \text{Random}$$

Multiplicative Model

$$\text{Series} = \text{Trend} \times \text{Seasonal} \times \text{Random}$$

Linear regression and correlation

The linear regression equation of y on x is given by:

$$Y = a + bX \quad \text{or} \quad Y - \bar{Y} = b(X - \bar{X})$$

Financial Mathematics

Compound Interest (Values and Sums)

Future Value of S, of a sum X, invested for n periods, compounded at $r\%$ interest

$$S = X[1 + r]^n$$

Annuity

Present value of an annuity of £1 per annum receivable or payable for n years, commencing in one year, discounted at $r\%$ per annum.

$$PV = \frac{1}{r}\left[1 - \frac{1}{[1 + r]^n}\right]$$

Perpetuity

Present value of £1 per annum, payable or receivable in perpetuity, commencing in one year, discounted at $r\%$ per annum.

$$PV = \frac{1}{r}$$

Note that logarithm tables are also available when you sit your assessment.

Probability

$A \cup B = A$ **or** B. $A \cap B = A$ **and** B (overlap). $P(B/A) =$ probability of B, **given** A.

Rules of addition

If A and B are *mutually exclusive*: $P(A \cup B) = P(A) + P(B)$
If A and B are **not** mutually exclusive: $P(A \cup B) = P(A) + P(B) - P(A \cap B)$

Rules of multiplication

If A and B are *independent*: $P(A \cap B) = P(A) \times P(B)$
If A and B are **not** independent: $P(A \cap B) = P(A) \times P(B/A)$

$E(X) =$ expected value $=$ probability $\times$ payoff

Quadratic equations

If $aX^2 + bX + c = 0$ is the general quadratic equation, then the two solutions (roots) are given by

$$X = \frac{-b \pm \sqrt{b^2 - 4ac}}{2a}$$

Index numbers

Price relative $= 100 \times P_1/P_0$

Quantity relative $= 100 \times Q_1/Q_0$

Price: $\dfrac{\Sigma W \times P_1/P_0}{\Sigma W} \times 100$ where W denotes weights

Quantity: $\dfrac{\Sigma W \times Q_1/Q_0}{\Sigma W} \times 100$ where W denotes weights

Coefficient of correlation (r)

$$r = \frac{\text{Covariance } (XY)}{\sqrt{\text{VAR } (X).\text{VAR } (Y)}}$$

$$= \frac{n \sum XY - (\sum X)(\sum Y)}{\sqrt{[n \sum X^2 - (\sum X)^2][n \sum Y^2 - (\sum Y)^2]}}$$

$$R(\text{rank}) = 1 - \left[\frac{6 \sum d^2}{n(n^2 - 1)} \right]$$

Mathematical tables

Present value table

Present value of £1, i.e. $(1+r) - n$ where $r =$ interest rate, $n =$ number of periods until payment or receipt.

Periods	Interest rates (r)									
(n)	1%	2%	3%	4%	5%	6%	7%	8%	9%	10%
1	0.990	0.980	0.971	0.962	0.952	0.943	0.935	0.926	0.917	0.909
2	0.980	0.961	0.943	0.925	0.907	0.890	0.873	0.857	0.842	0.826
3	0.971	0.942	0.915	0.889	0.864	0.840	0.816	0.794	0.772	0.751
4	0.961	0.924	0.888	0.855	0.823	0.792	0.763	0.735	0.708	0.683
5	0.951	0.906	0.863	0.822	0.784	0.747	0.713	0.681	0.650	0.621
6	0.942	0.888	0.837	0.790	0.746	0.705	0.666	0.630	0.596	0.564
7	0.933	0.871	0.813	0.760	0.711	0.665	0.623	0.583	0.547	0.513
8	0.923	0.853	0.789	0.731	0.677	0.627	0.582	0.540	0.502	0.467
9	0.914	0.837	0.766	0.703	0.645	0.592	0.544	0.500	0.460	0.424
10	0.905	0.820	0.744	0.676	0.614	0.558	0.508	0.463	0.422	0.386
11	0.896	0.804	0.722	0.650	0.585	0.527	0.475	0.429	0.388	0.350
12	0.887	0.788	0.701	0.625	0.557	0.497	0.444	0.397	0.356	0.319
13	0.879	0.773	0.681	0.601	0.530	0.469	0.415	0.368	0.326	0.290
14	0.870	0.758	0.661	0.577	0.505	0.442	0.388	0.340	0.299	0.263
15	0.861	0.743	0.642	0.555	0.481	0.417	0.362	0.315	0.275	0.239
16	0.853	0.728	0.623	0.534	0.458	0.394	0.339	0.292	0.252	0.218
17	0.844	0.714	0.605	0.513	0.436	0.371	0.317	0.270	0.231	0.198
18	0.836	0.700	0.587	0.494	0.416	0.350	0.296	0.250	0.212	0.180
19	0.828	0.686	0.570	0.475	0.396	0.331	0.277	0.232	0.194	0.164
20	0.820	0.673	0.554	0.456	0.377	0.312	0.258	0.215	0.178	0.149

Periods	Interest rates (r)									
(n)	11%	12%	13%	14%	15%	16%	17%	18%	19%	20%
1	0.901	0.893	0.885	0.877	0.870	0.862	0.855	0.847	0.840	0.833
2	0.812	0.797	0.783	0.769	0.756	0.743	0.731	0.718	0.706	0.694
3	0.731	0.712	0.693	0.675	0.658	0.641	0.624	0.609	0.593	0.579
4	0.659	0.636	0.613	0.592	0.572	0.552	0.534	0.516	0.499	0.482
5	0.593	0.567	0.543	0.519	0.497	0.476	0.456	0.437	0.419	0.402
6	0.535	0.507	0.480	0.456	0.432	0.410	0.390	0.370	0.352	0.335
7	0.482	0.452	0.425	0.400	0.376	0.354	0.333	0.314	0.296	0.279
8	0.434	0.404	0.376	0.351	0.327	0.305	0.285	0.266	0.249	0.233
9	0.391	0.361	0.333	0.308	0.284	0.263	0.243	0.225	0.209	0.194
10	0.352	0.322	0.295	0.270	0.247	0.227	0.208	0.191	0.176	0.162
11	0.317	0.287	0.261	0.237	0.215	0.195	0.178	0.162	0.148	0.135
12	0.286	0.257	0.231	0.208	0.187	0.168	0.152	0.137	0.124	0.112
13	0.258	0.229	0.204	0.182	0.163	0.145	0.130	0.116	0.104	0.093
14	0.232	0.205	0.181	0.160	0.141	0.125	0.111	0.099	0.088	0.078
15	0.209	0.183	0.160	0.140	0.123	0.108	0.095	0.084	0.074	0.065
16	0.188	0.163	0.141	0.123	0.107	0.093	0.081	0.071	0.062	0.054
17	0.170	0.146	0.125	0.108	0.093	0.080	0.069	0.060	0.052	0.045
18	0.153	0.130	0.111	0.095	0.081	0.069	0.059	0.051	0.044	0.038
19	0.138	0.116	0.098	0.083	0.070	0.060	0.051	0.043	0.037	0.031
20	0.124	0.104	0.087	0.073	0.061	0.051	0.043	0.037	0.031	0.026

Cumulative present value table

This table shows the present value of £1 per annum, receivable or payable at the end of each year for n years $\dfrac{1-(1+r)^{-n}}{r}$.

Periods	Interest rates (r)									
(n)	1%	2%	3%	4%	5%	6%	7%	8%	9%	10%
1	0.990	0.980	0.971	0.962	0.952	0.943	0.935	0.926	0.917	0.909
2	1.970	1.942	1.913	1.886	1.859	1.833	1.808	1.783	1.759	1.736
3	2.941	2.834	2.829	2.775	2.723	2.673	2.624	2.577	2.531	2.487
4	3.902	3.808	3.717	3.630	3.546	3.465	3.387	3.312	3.240	3.170
5	4.853	4.713	4.580	4.452	4.329	4.212	4.100	3.993	3.890	3.791
6	5.795	5.601	5.417	5.242	5.076	4.917	4.767	4.623	4.486	4.355
7	6.728	6.472	6.230	6.002	5.786	5.582	5.389	5.206	5.033	4.868
8	7.652	7.325	7.020	6.733	6.463	6.210	5.971	5.747	5.535	5.335
9	8.566	8.162	7.786	7.435	7.108	6.802	6.515	6.247	5.995	5.759
10	9.471	8.983	8.530	8.111	7.722	7.360	7.024	6.710	6.418	6.145
11	10.368	9.787	9.253	8.760	8.306	7.887	7.499	7.139	6.805	6.495
12	11.255	10.575	9.954	9.385	8.863	8.384	7.943	7.536	7.161	6.814
13	12.134	11.348	10.635	9.986	9.394	8.853	8.358	7.904	7.487	7.103
14	13.004	12.106	11.296	10.563	9.899	9.295	8.745	8.244	7.786	7.367
15	13.865	12.849	11.938	11.118	10.380	9.712	9.108	8.559	8.061	7.606
16	14.718	13.578	12.561	11.652	10.838	10.106	9.447	8.851	8.313	7.824
17	15.562	14.292	13.166	12.166	11.274	10.477	9.763	9.122	8.544	8.022
18	16.398	14.992	13.754	12.659	11.690	10.828	10.059	9.372	8.756	8.201
19	17.226	15.679	14.324	13.134	12.085	11.158	10.336	9.604	8.950	8.365
20	18.046	16.351	14.878	13.590	12.462	11.470	10.594	9.818	9.129	8.514

Periods	Interest rates (r)									
(n)	11%	12%	13%	14%	15%	16%	17%	18%	19%	20%
1	0.901	0.893	0.885	0.877	0.870	0.862	0.855	0.847	0.840	0.833
2	1.713	1.690	1.668	1.647	1.626	1.605	1.585	1.566	1.547	1.528
3	2.444	2.402	2.361	2.322	2.283	2.246	2.210	2.174	2.140	2.106
4	3.102	3.037	2.974	2.914	2.855	2.798	2.743	2.690	2.639	2.589
5	3.696	3.605	3.517	3.433	3.352	3.274	3.199	3.127	3.058	2.991
6	4.231	4.111	3.998	3.889	3.784	3.685	3.589	3.498	3.410	3.326
7	4.712	4.564	4.423	4.288	4.160	4.039	3.922	3.812	3.706	3.605
8	5.146	4.968	4.799	4.639	4.487	4.344	4.207	4.078	3.954	3.837
9	5.537	5.328	5.132	4.946	4.772	4.607	4.451	4.303	4.163	4.031
10	5.889	5.650	5.426	5.216	5.019	4.833	4.659	4.494	4.339	4.192
11	6.207	5.938	5.687	5.453	5.234	5.029	4.836	4.656	4.486	4.327
12	6.492	6.194	5.918	5.660	5.421	5.197	4.988	4.793	4.611	4.439
13	6.750	6.424	6.122	5.842	5.583	5.342	5.118	4.910	4.715	4.533
14	6.982	6.628	6.302	6.002	5.724	5.468	5.229	5.008	4.802	4.611
15	7.191	6.811	6.462	6.142	5.847	5.575	5.324	5.092	4.876	4.675
16	7.379	6.974	6.604	6.265	5.954	5.668	5.405	5.162	4.938	4.730
17	7.549	7.120	6.729	6.373	6.047	5.749	5.475	5.222	4.990	4.775
18	7.702	7.250	6.840	6.467	6.128	5.818	5.534	5.273	5.033	4.812
19	7.839	7.366	6.938	6.550	6.198	5.877	5.584	5.316	5.070	4.843
20	7.963	7.469	7.025	6.623	6.259	5.929	5.628	5.353	5.101	4.870

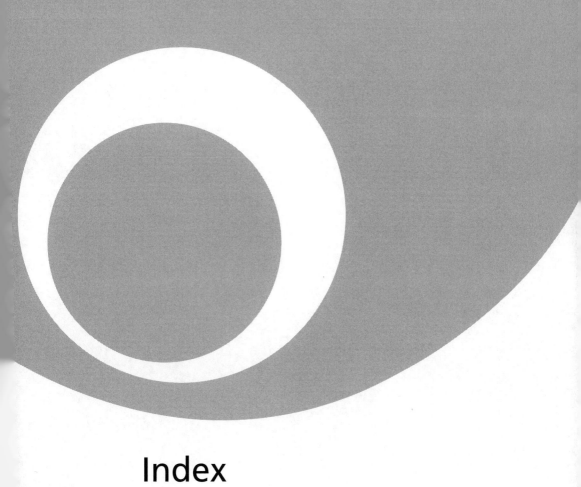

Index